ANCIENT MYTHS & LEGENDS
WITHOUT MEN

Ancient Myths & Legends *Without Men*

Mara Gold

INTRODUCTION 09

¹⁸ Family Tree

Homemaker ²⁴
GAIA, RHEA, DEMETER AND PERSEPHONE,
PANDORA, PASIPHAË, LAMIA

⁶² Virgin
ATHENA, ARTEMIS, HESTIA

Warrior ⁸⁸
AMAZONS, SRIKANDI, ATALANTA,
JOAN OF ARC, VALKYRIES, SEKHMET

114 Femme Fatale
APHRODITE, HELEN OF TROY,
CLYTEMNESTRA, CALYPSO

Witch 144
HECATE, MEDEA, CIRCE,
KURANGAITUKU

Madwoman 172
MAENADS, WOMEN OF LEMNOS,
FURIES, CASSANDRA, HERA

194 Monster
MEDUSA, CETO, SCYLLA AND
CHARYBDIS, SIRENS VS MERMAIDS,
ECHIDNA, CHIMERA, SPHINX

CONCLUSION 228,
ACKNOWLEDGEMENTS 230, INDEX 234

Introduction

The women of ancient mythology and legends were always put in their place – whether on a pedestal or in the shadows. Cast as virtuous mothers, seductive threats or outright monsters, their stories were rarely, if ever, their own. Mythological women were often blamed for the misfortunes of men but in reality, women in the ancient world held very little power. Over time, women living across the world have reclaimed many of these myths, and in them have found strong female role models whose legacies have survived, independent of men.

Although the title of this book is *Ancient Myths & Legends Without Men*, it is almost impossible to discuss the women of mythology without including any men in their stories at all. This is because Greek society was male-focused, and women tended to be portrayed as either villains against or victims of men. Breaking with the traditional tellings of these tales, this book will centre these women in their own stories, where previously they were relegated as a sidenote to a hero's victory or the cause of his tragedy.

The archetypes which form the organising principle of this book – Homemaker, Virgin, Warrior, Femme Fatale, Witch, Madwoman and Monster – have both fascinated and repulsed women in the centuries since they were created, and have been taken up by those looking for a feminist understanding of ancient mythology. Each of the archetypes represents a scale of acceptable to unacceptable womanhood in varying degrees. This book will explore how these archetypes have evolved, and how what they mean has shifted in significance in the years since they were created. In many cases, the more antithetic a character was to 'acceptable' womanhood, the more heroic she has now become to contemporary feminists. Medusa, who graces our cover, was once a symbol of an imagined threat to male domination but now is understood by feminist writers and readers for who she really was – a sexual assault survivor whose rage was truly justified.

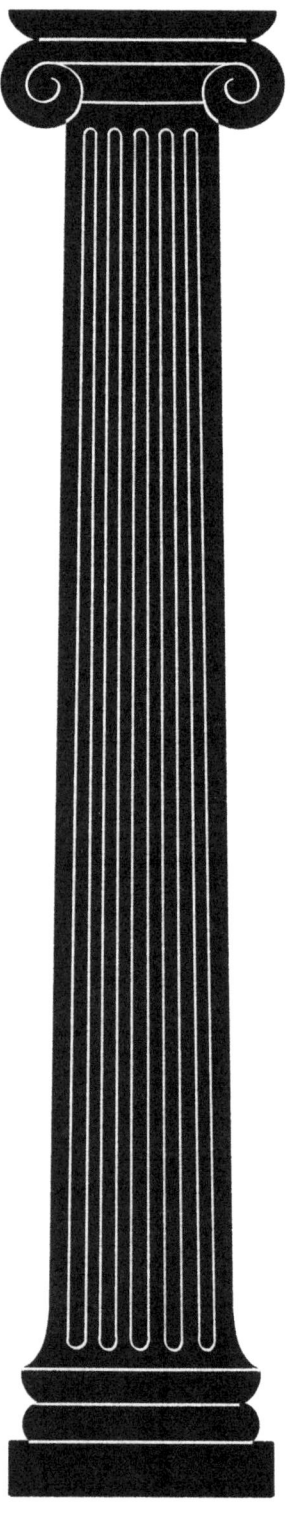

This does not mean that Medusa isn't still seen as the original 'nasty woman' of the ancient world, particularly by supporters of the patriarchy. Today, the image of Medusa is still used as a slur, with female politicians like Hilary Clinton often portrayed as Medusa online and in right-wing media. The fact that the same misogyny of the classical world survives in our modern one and is weaponised to attack very real women today shows how important it is for us to understand ancient archetypes of womanhood, to discover the truth of their stories, and to set about reclaiming these stories to empower women today.

Whilst we know that the lives of the women described on the pages of this book might be more fiction than fact, mythology has always been a useful way for those whose stories are not represented in traditional histories to build their own heritage. Traditional history books of the classical world have largely focused on cis straight men, mainly because the sexist, highly patriarchal societies of ancient Greece and Rome regularly left women out of the official narrative. As a result, mythology is an interesting place to search for clues regarding the lives of ancient women, often hidden in what is left unsaid. Sometimes, in looking at how the actions of mythological woman provide an example of what not to do, we can piece together the strict standards and rules under which ancient women (particularly those in Greece) had to live.

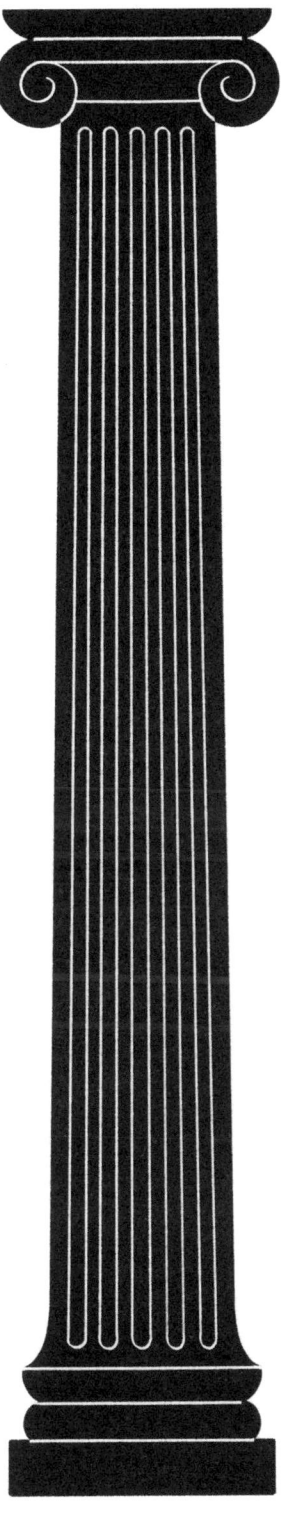

Within ancient mythology, not only are there tales that many cis women can relate to but also trans and queer readings of these stories. The classical world did not have the same understanding of sexuality and gender as we do today, or even a word for homosexuality. Certain practices that we would describe as queer today were a normal part of classical society and therefore appear in mythology. Some historical figures, like the poet Sappho from Lesbos, have been mythologised to the point that we now cannot accurately separate fact from fiction. Crucially, how women have interpreted mythology and mythologised history has changed over time. Every artistic and literary engagement with these women's stories adds a new layer of meaning to them, making these ancient myths and legends living, breathing records of what it means to be a woman over the past two thousand years. In Academia, this is called 'Classical Reception'. In reality, what this means is that mythology is still alive and ever-evolving, added to by women across many centuries, including ourselves.

This book examines the primary female archetypes of classical mythology, with some comparisons to mythologies from other cultures, and delves into views of women in the ancient world and how these views have changed (or in many cases how they haven't) in the centuries since. We will encounter good mothers and bad mothers; femme fatales and seductresses; maniacs and madwomen; beasts and monsters; warriors and athletes; maidens and spinsters; witches and sorceresses. Many of the women could easily fit into multiple categories, but they are placed according to their role within their own stories. It is not meant to be a comprehensive encyclopedia of all women in myth and legend, although there is a very handy family tree on p.18-23, but rather an introduction to the essential archetypes of ancient womanhood through the women that best exemplify them. Their stories echo through time, as they are continually reinterpreted and retold as models of womanhood, particularly through feminist activism and culture today.

Even if you might not learn about every mythological woman, you will hopefully gain an understanding of the inextricable link between mythology and women's lives, both then and now.

Please note: if you are not familiar with classical mythology, please be aware that sexual assault and violence against women is unfortunately commonplace. This book does not obscure these stories as they are important in understanding the reception of these myths over the years and the survivor narratives that have recently replaced the idea of women as victims in modern times. Often, these grisly beginnings originated the feminist rage our mythological women now represent.

Family

Tree

The family tree on the following pages gives an overview of how women in Greek mythology were connected to one another. Traditionally family trees follow the male line, but this often obscures the connections between women, and prevents us from understanding the female perspective.

Since this book does not attempt to cover all the mythological women you might have heard of, this family tree fills in some of the gaps and highlights female legacies that are not immediately obvious. This tree includes characters that are not featured in the book to show how they are related to famous heroines or supposed villains. There are also names included within the book, but not included on the tree because they were not connected to established mythological families or were purposely fashioned by the gods, like Pandora.

You will also notice that the tree might have multiple options for parentage because of the multiple versions of each myth. Mythology always has and always will be messy, failing to fit into neat boxes or in this case, trees, but it is still important to try and make sense of it, even if we do so in our own ways.

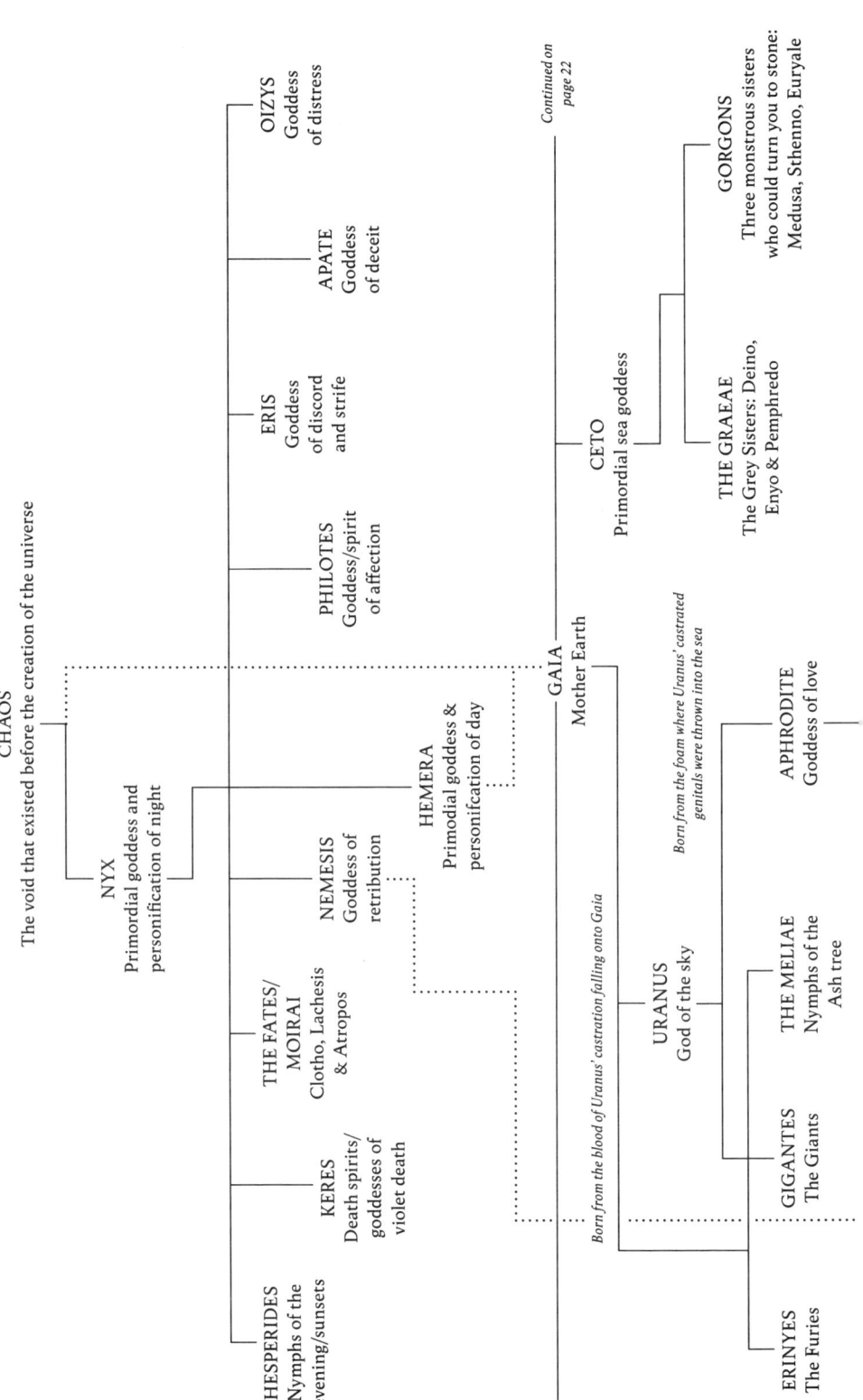

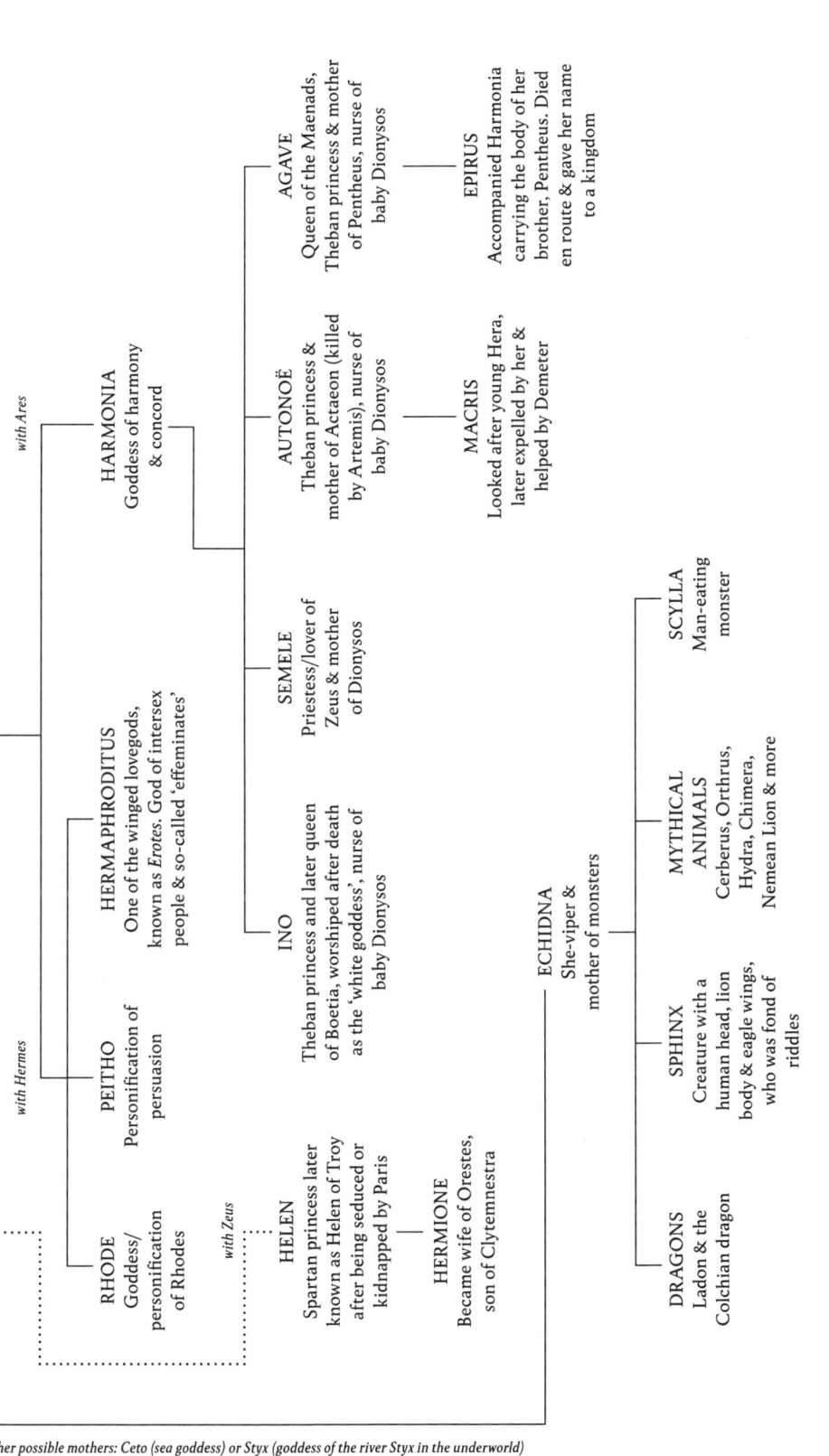

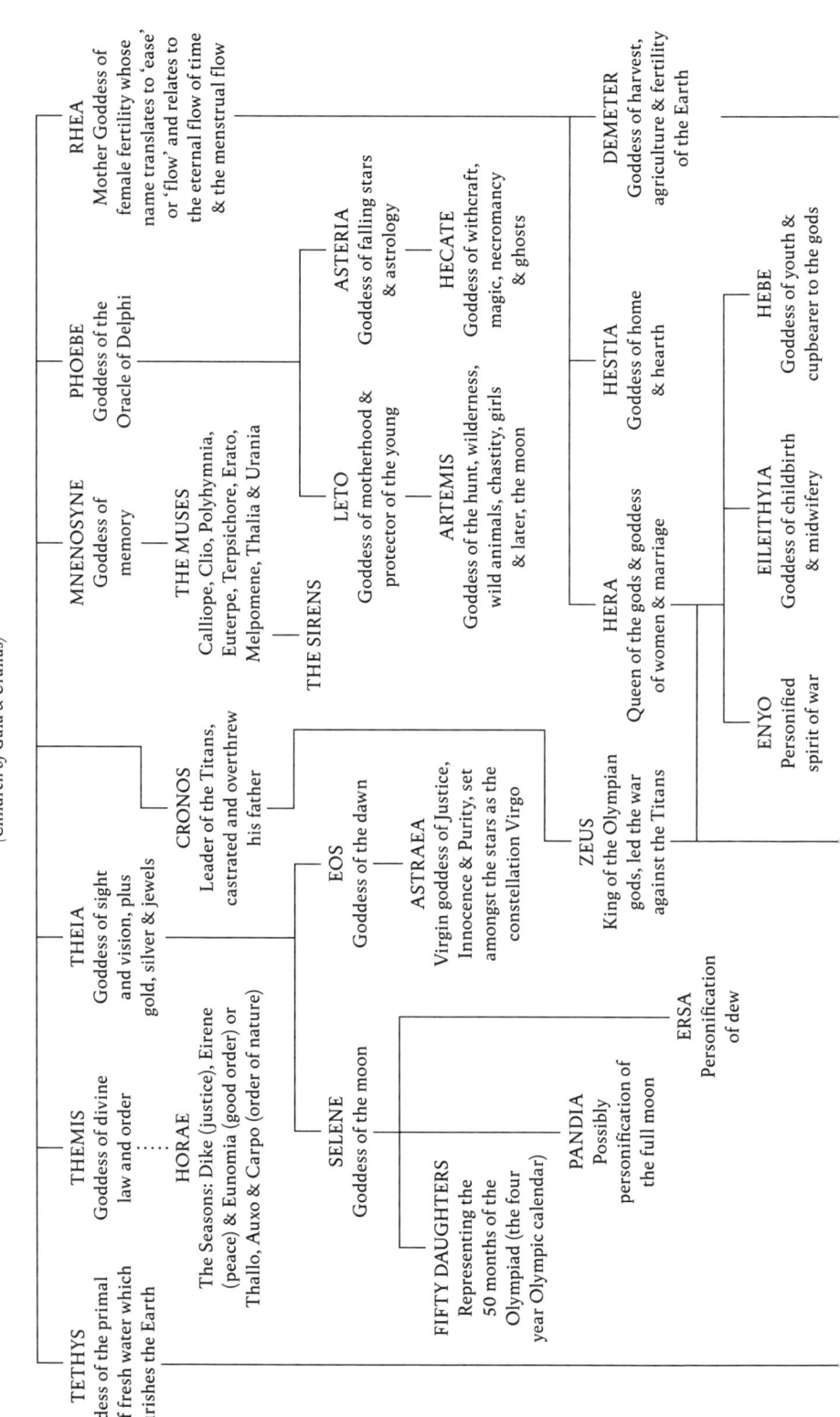

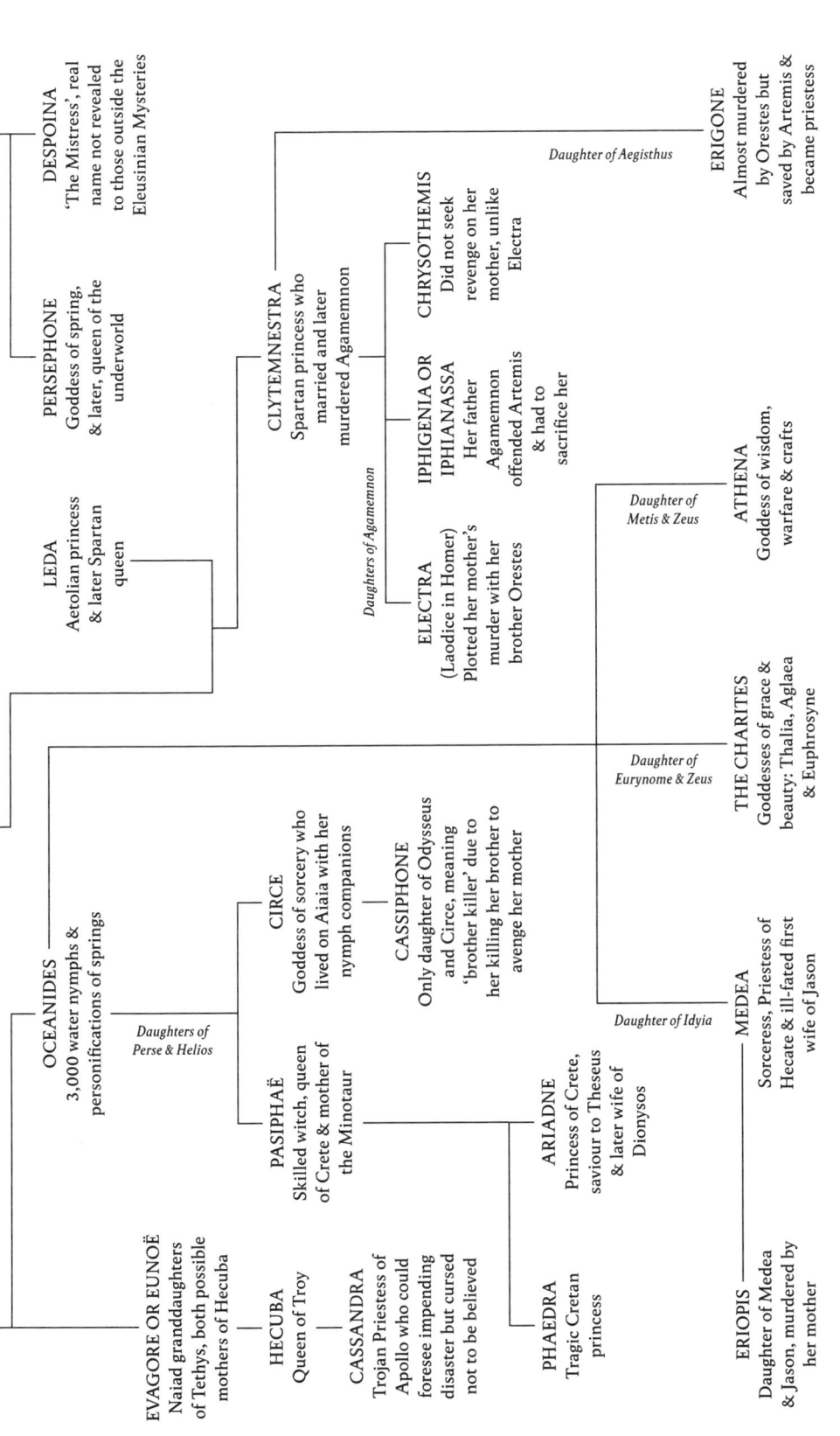

Homemaker

Homemaking was the only acceptable path for women in Greece and Rome, to the point that it was actually considered dangerous for women's bodies and sanity not to reproduce. Mythological wives and mothers reinforced the strictly segregated gender roles practised in the ancient world and underlined the household as women's domain. In classical Athens, women had no legal status and lived under their husbands' authority – though they would likely spend little time together. Women mostly stayed indoors and could not participate in public life, but fulfilled their duty by producing male heirs and citizens.

Women's bodies were severely misunderstood in the ancient world, causing women to rely on a combination of questionable medical practices and religious beliefs. Most women's health issues were blamed on the uterus, which was thought to wander the body when not functioning correctly. The 'medical cure' for many women's ailments was pregnancy and marriage, as empty wombs were likely to dry out and/or wander around the body, causing all manner of problems, including some such as suffocation. Unmarried women were considered at risk of suffering hallucinations or throwing themselves down a well. This is where we get the concept of 'hysteria' from, with the word itself coming from the Greek word for 'uterus'.

The original mother goddesses tell us more about how Greeks understood natural phenomena and the world around them than they do about the powerless position of real historical mothers, as their voices were rarely recorded in historical sources. As we will see, these contrasting tales of homemakers also offers insight into what *men* believed marriage and motherhood should (and shouldn't) look like.

GAIA

The mother of all mothers, Gaia (or Terra in Latin) was the goddess of the Earth. She was born at the beginning of time, second only to her brother Chaos. She gave birth to three sons without any man involved (known as parthenogenesis). One of those sons was Uranus, god of the sky, to whom she was also married and bore eighteen more children: the Titans and the Cyclopes (a race of one-eyed giants) and three Hecatoncheires (Hundred-Handers). By mating with the sea, she bore the sea gods. She conceived the Giants with Tartarus, the Greek equivalent to hell. She was grandmother to Medusa and her Gorgon sisters, who were the children of her daughter Ceto (see page 204).

Uranus hated the monstrous Cyclopes and Hecatoncheires because they were so hideous to look at. He hid them within Gaia's body (the belly of the Earth) without her consent, causing her agony. She begged her Titan children to help her retaliate. Only Cronos, her youngest and most terrible, agreed. Gaia invited Uranus to sleep with her whilst Cronos lay in wait. He ambushed his father, castrating him with a diamond sickle Gaia had given him. Uranus' blood and genitalia falling upon the sea and Earth created new life, including the Erinyes or Furies (see page 183) and Aphrodite (page 117).

Today, modern pagan movements worship Gaia as Mother Earth or the spiritual embodiment of Earth, including Wicca. You might also see her name appear on health food brands and organic products or in eco-feminist theory. Her Latin name, Terra, is an alternate name for Earth, and a popular trope in Science Fiction. Most Alien races in the *Marvel Cinematic Universe* refer to Earth as Terra and humans as Terrans. She has a place setting under the name 'Primordial Goddess' on feminist artist Judy Chicago's spectacular installation *The Dinner Party*, representing a table and place settings for some of the most iconic (and rule-breaking) women from mythology and history. Created collaboratively between 1974 and 1979, the installation is now housed in the excellent Elizabeth A. Sackler Center for Feminist Art at the Brooklyn Museum. The Primordial Goddess' setting celebrates early women's crafts, like basket-weaving, pottery and clothes-making, whilst her plate evokes both flesh and rock to symbolise the eternal link between women and Mother Earth. Gaia was often worshipped in association with Demeter/Ceres (see page 34).

HOMEMAKER

RHEA

She is lesser known today, but Rhea was the mother of many of the most famous and celebrated gods. She is known as the mother of gods or the great Mother and represented the flow of time, menstrual blood, birth waters and milk. Her name means 'ease' or 'flow,' which she was also the goddess of. She bore five Olympian gods: Demeter, Hera, Hestia, Poseidon and Zeus; as well as Hades, god of the underworld. However, motherhood did not come easy – their father Cronos heard a prophecy that his children would overthrow him, so he swallowed each child the moment they were born. Grief-stricken, Rhea eventually devised a plan with the help of her parents (Gaia and Uranus), giving Cronos a rock to swallow instead of their youngest child, Zeus. She whisked Zeus away, hiding him on Crete until he was old enough to defeat Cronos and rescue his siblings by making his father regurgitate them. Rhea retired from her role as queen to focus on being a mother and grandmother once Zeus became king of the gods. Some classical texts, like the *Homeric Hymn to Demeter*, highlight her role as mother of gods, particularly in her relationship with her daughter Demeter. After Demeter's daughter (and Rhea's granddaughter) was forced to marry Hades, Rhea helped Demeter to resolve her anger and return to Olympus with the other principal gods. As a devoted grandmother, she attended the birth of multiple grandchildren, including Apollo and Dionysos. Rhea raised Dionysos until his teenage years in Lydia (modern-day Turkey) and also eased a madness inflicted on Dionysos by Hera. She sometimes joined in with the ecstatic dances of Dionysos' Maenads, whose number included her sister Agave (see page 178). She had several temples in Greece dedicated to her under the name 'Mother of the Gods'. She was later assimilated with the Anatolian mother goddess, Cybele, another model of ideal maternal devotion.

DEMETER AND PERSEPHONE

One of the most famous mythological mothers, Demeter is remembered for causing the changing seasons out of grief for her daughter, Persephone. Persephone was famously kidnapped (or in some stories wooed) by Hades, king of the underworld. Unaware of her daughter's whereabouts, Demeter furiously searched the Earth looking for her until she learnt of Persephone's kidnap. She was devastated. Overflowing with grief and rage, she neglected her divine duties as goddess of the harvest and agriculture, resulting in famine and death. Demeter begged Zeus, who was Persephone's father, to return their daughter. But Persephone had already eaten a food of the underworld, a pomegranate seed, which meant that she could not leave according to Hades' rules. Demeter and Zeus negotiated with Hades and came to a compromise: Persephone would spend six months of the year in the underworld and six months on Earth. Each time Persephone returned to her mother, Demeter would rejoice, making the crops, flowers and other plants flourish. But when her daughter descended back to the Underworld, plants would wither and die. Persephone's myth was used to explain the changing of the seasons from spring and summer to autumn and winter.

HOMEMAKER

One of the great pieces of early ancient Greek literature tells the story of Demeter in a very unique way: the *Homeric Hymn to Demeter*. It focuses on a woman's perspective and feelings, which was extremely unusual in a male-dominated medium, leading some feminist scholars to believe that the author could have been a woman. Demeter's emotions shine through in the lyrical hymn, which tells the story of her daughter's abduction and her fight to win her back. The hymn explores the goddess' stages of grief, from 'Unsmiling, not partaking of food or drink/she sat there, wasting away with yearning for her daughter,' to making that year 'the most terrible one for mortals,' by nearly destroying the entire race of humans with 'harsh hunger.' It also gives scholars an insight into an ancient woman's experiences, particularly that of motherhood, age and class. Not only does the hymn describe Demeter's grief in detail, it also gives us an insight into raising children as a mortal woman. In her search for Persephone on Earth, Demeter disguised herself as an old woman and became nursemaid to the son of the king and queen of Eleusis. This tells us both about childcare for wealthy women and the types of roles pushed onto older, poorer women. The hymn also refers to the foundation of Eleusis as a sacred site, with Demeter directly instructing Metaneira (the queen) on buildings and rituals to honour her. Though these rituals remained secret, it shows that worship at Eleusis was not just focused on a goddess, but that its mythological history was female-centred. Because the *Hymn* allows us a glimpse into women's lives in ancient Greece, many women writers, scholars and performers have been drawn to it. It was a popular performance subject in women's colleges at the turn of the twentieth century.

Demeter came from a line of mother goddesses, as Rhea's daughter and Gaia's granddaughter. Demeter herself was known as 'Grain-Mother' and 'Earth-Mother' to the ancient Greeks. Demeter and Persephone represented both fertility and death and were at the centre of a major religious cult known as the Eleusinian Mysteries, which is located at Eleusis, a sanctuary that you can still visit today. The Demeter–Persephone myth is used today to interpret and understand mother-daughter relationships and was particularly important during the late nineteenth and early twentieth century to explain the generational gap between old-fashioned mothers and the so-called 'modern daughter' who wished to be educated and independent. The women of Somerville College, who were trying to justify their place at the University of Oxford, staged an original production based on Demeter and Persephone in 1904 as part of a celebration of women's education and the opening of the first purpose-built library at an Oxford women's college. Entitled *Demeter*, the production equated the underworld with knowledge and Persephone's journey with a woman's college years, helping promote women's education in the hostile environment of a traditionally male-only university. At the end of the play, Demeter realises she will never quite understand what Persephone has seen, experienced and heard, but they can still maintain a loving relationship through compromise.

Today, Persephone is the more popular figure, appearing frequently in literature, graphic novels, film and television, theatre and music. Mary Shelley penned a drama about her (published posthumously) entitled *Proserpine*, she appears in her queen of the underworld guise in Syfy's *The Magicians* as well as Netflix's *KAOS*, she inspired *A Court of Mist and Fury* by Sarah J. Maas, and she stars in Anaïs Mitchell's musical *Hadestown*. She also lends her name to Persephone Books, a British publisher focused on reprinting women writers from the late nineteenth and early twentieth centuries – the same period that Persephone herself had a renaissance.

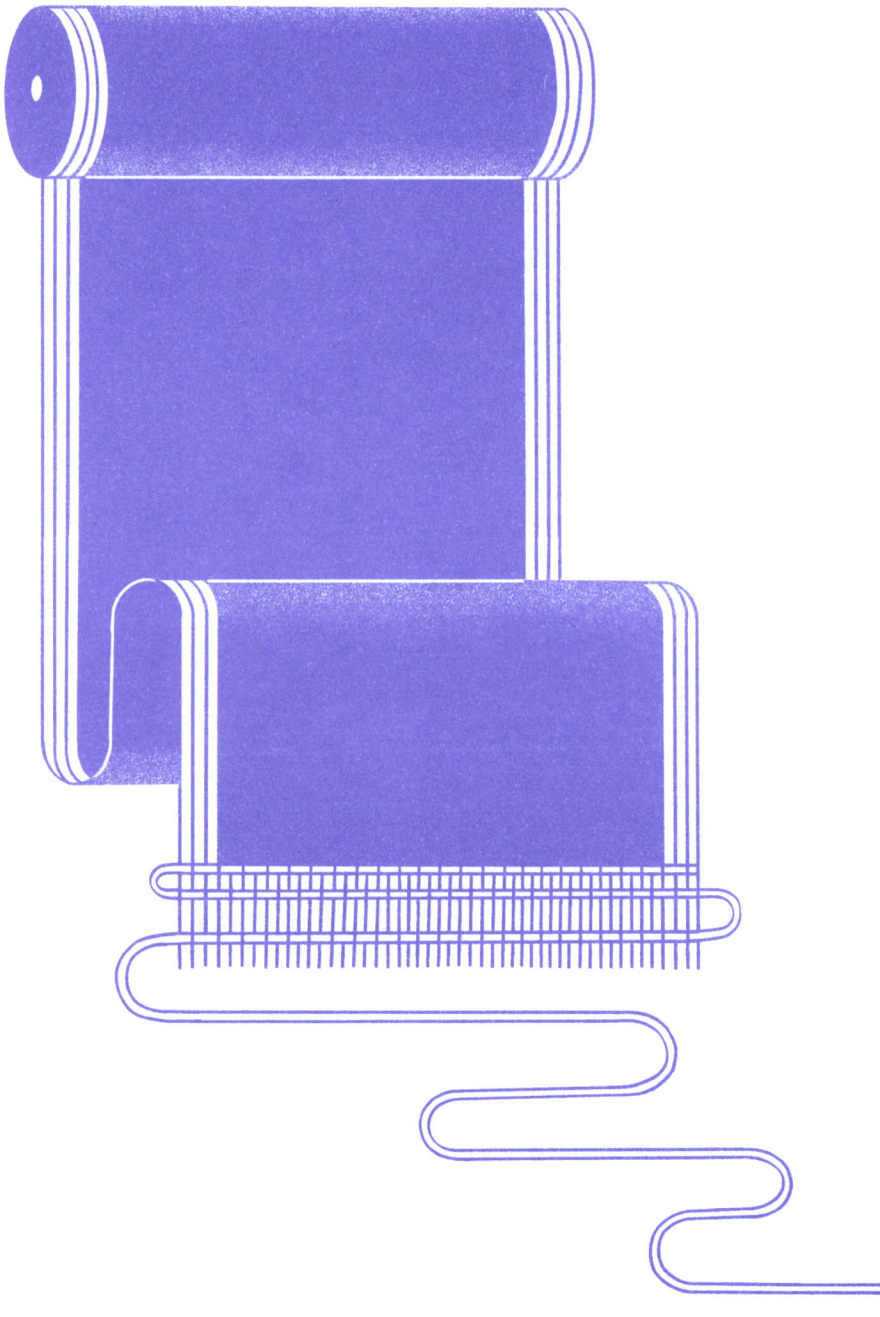

PENELOPE: THE PERFECT WIFE

Penelope was rewarded for her loyalty to her husband Odysseus and her dedication to her son Telemachus. She remained faithful to Odysseus and deceived prospective suitors in his long absence during and after the Trojan War, waiting two decades for his return without giving up hope that he was alive. Despite only having a brief amount of time together before Odysseus left for the Trojan War, Penelope's loyalty was unwavering, and she raised their son according to Odysseus' ideals. She is depicted as the ideal Greek woman – a faithful wife with accomplished domestic skills – in contrast to those wives and mothers who are ultimately punished for stepping outside of their assigned role as a woman in the domestic realm, like Clytemnestra, another wife left behind during the Trojan war (see page 132). In folk traditions, Penelope quite literally means 'weft-face' a suitable name for a woman skilled in both weaving and deceiving.

Penelope is one of the few 'good' women in the *Odyssey* and is shown as a positive example of womanhood, whilst also emphasising the negative traits of 'bad' women, like Circe or Calypso (see pages 138 and 160), by contrast. She was clever within her domain of domesticity but not too clever for a woman. During Odysseus' twenty-year absence, Penelope drew the attention of over a hundred suitors, who all moved into the royal palace and pressured her to remarry. According to the highly valued conventions of hospitality in ancient Greece, Penelope had no choice but to receive them as guests. However, these suitors were a rowdy bunch and asserted a degree of power over the household, drinking and eating their supplies and harassing the women, simply because the man of the house was away and they also happened to be men. Penelope is shown to be a good host, and the suitors' appalling behaviour serves to amplify Penelope and Odysseus' virtues.

HOMEMAKER

Odysseus' patron goddess Athena pressured Penelope to appear to the suitors so she might fan the flames of their desire, therefore making her even more attractive to Odysseus due to her sexual value and her loyalty to him. Odysseus was known to be particularly cunning in traditionally masculine pursuits such as war and diplomacy; Penelope was similarly cunning inside the home and used her mastery of domestic arts to trick the suitors. Penelope's domestic skills were considered 'feminine' by the Greeks and play an important role in the *Odyssey* to highlight her suitability as the wife of such a clever hero. She used her feminine wiles to delay her suitors by promising to select one when she finished weaving a shroud. But every night, she unpicked most of her day's work and redid it the following day, never making any progress. Unlike Circe and Calypso, who used unnatural talents (like enchantments and concealment) to keep Odysseus, Penelope used her natural womanly skills (like weaving) to keep other men away. This lasted for three years until one of her maids betrayed her to the suitors. Apparently, some of Penelope's maids had been sleeping with the suitors, providing another point of contrast to Penelope's goodness.

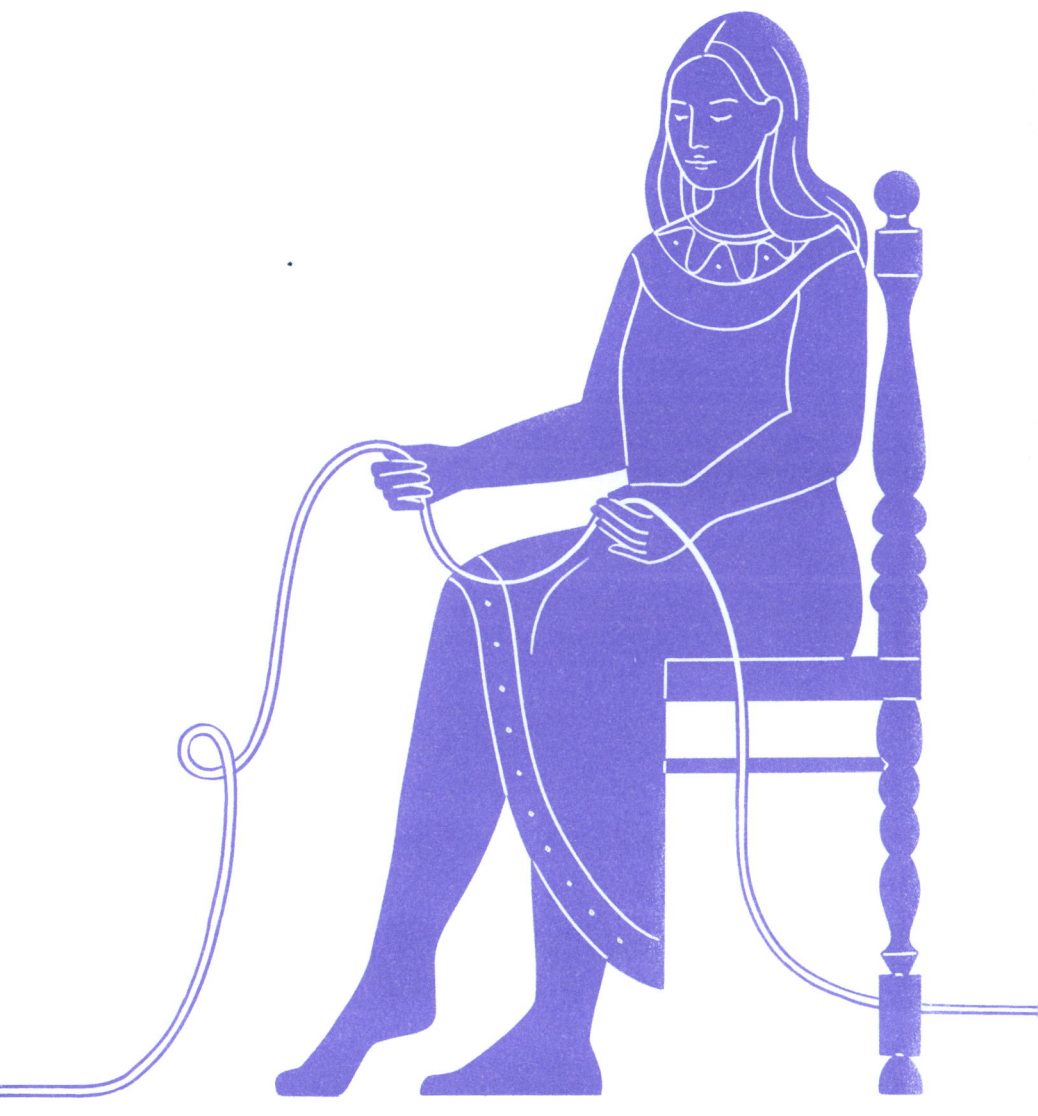

HOMEMAKER

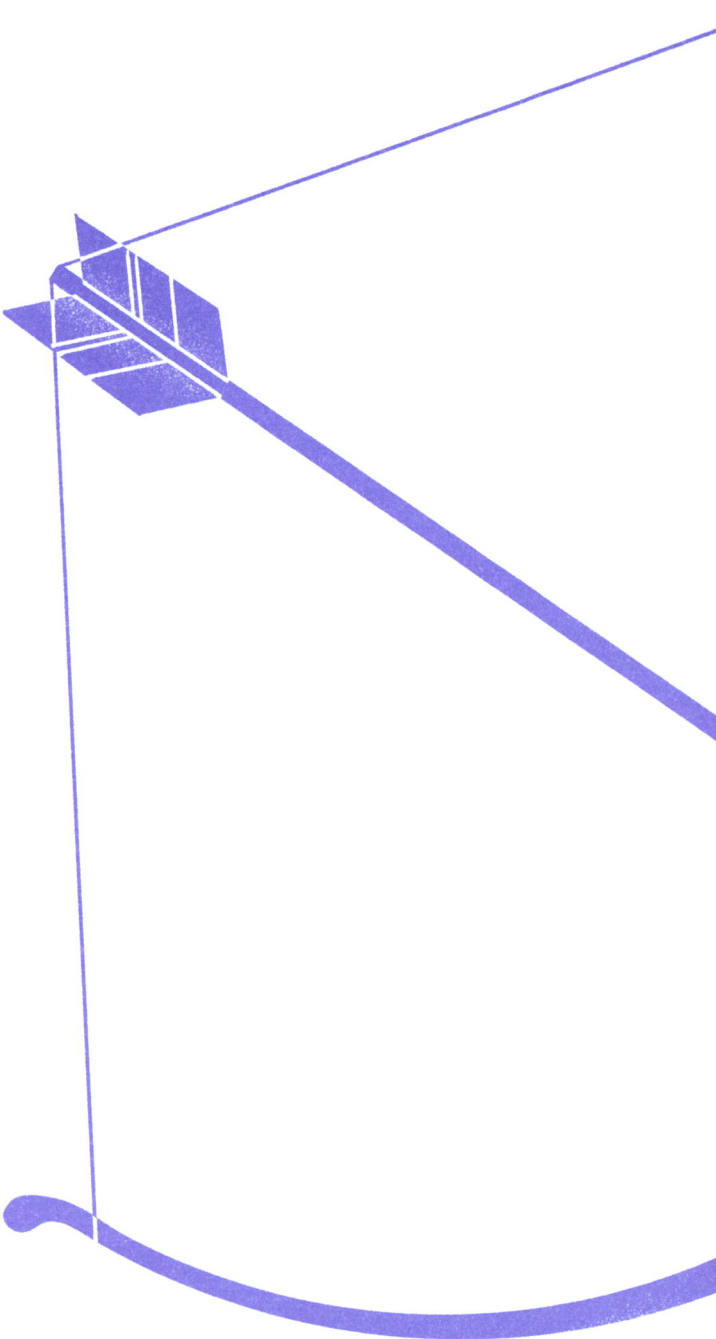

HOMEMAKER

After many years, Odysseus eventually returns home disguised as an old man in order to spy on what had been happening in his absence. The estranged couple have a long conversation, during which Odysseus (still in disguise) claims he met Odysseus when his ship was blown off course, overwhelming Penelope with emotion. Before their conversation comes to an end, she announces the idea of an archery competition, declaring that she will marry the man who can string Odysseus' bow and complete a feat of archery that only Odysseus could achieve: shooting an arrow through the hole in the middle of twelve axe heads, a near impossible task. Some scholars debate whether she was finally ready for a new hubsand or if this was simply another delay tactic. However, there is a strong case that Penelope was aware of the supposed old man's true identity and arranged the competition as an opportunity for Odysseus to reveal himself, solidifying her role as the ideal wife. Either way, the suitors aren't even able to string the bow so Odysseus wins, and he and Telemachus promptly kill all the suitors and Penelope's 'disloyal' maids. After some disbelief, Penelope is reunited with Odysseus and they live a long and happy life together. It was assumed she was happy and fulfilled because her husband returned to assert his control over the household. The End.

In stories beyond the *Odyssey*, Penelope is painted as a very different character – either sleeping with all one hundred and eight suitors or with one of the gods (either Hermes or Apollo in Greek literature, or Mercury in Latin sources) and giving birth to the god Pan. However, her reputation from the *Odyssey* is the most enduring, and by the Middle Ages, she was seen as an ongoing representation of the chaste wife. Margaret Atwood gave her and her murdered maids a voice in *The Penelopiad*, in which they tell their stories in hindsight and attempt to correct the misconceptions about them. The novel, which focusses on Penelope telling her life story from the underworld, also takes inspiration from Greek drama, portraying the maids as a Greek chorus (which also commonly consisted of twelve members). In theatre, the chorus usually represents the point of view of the general populace in the story or of the audience itself. However, Atwood has her maids interrupting Penelope with their own point of view in differing genres, from jump-rope rhymes to court trials. They compare their lives to that of their murderer, Telemachus, and blame Penelope for letting them die, tormenting both her and Odysseus in the underworld.

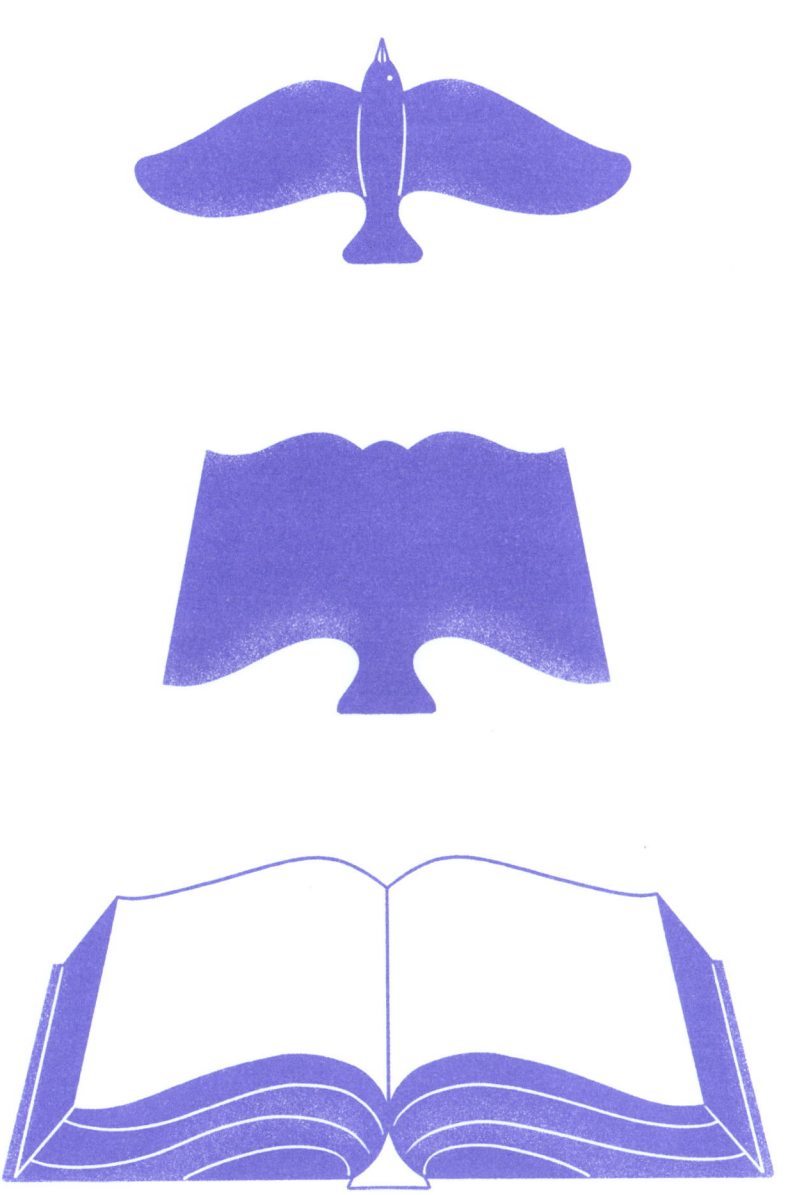

Mortal Mistakes

HOMEMAKER

PANDORA, THE MOTHER OF EVIL?

Pandora's story was devised to explain why evil exists in the world and, of course, it just had to be because of a woman. Her name can be translated as 'all-gifted' or 'all-giving' explaining both her creation and foreshadowing her role as the mother of humanity's downfall. You will likely have heard of Pandora's box and her inability to keep the damn thing closed, but as we will see, the trope of a 'bad' woman was actually a victim of the gods. The real story is this: Pandora was specifically created by the gods to punish humanity. Prometheus, one of the Titans, had stolen fire from the Olympians and given it to the race of men he had created. Zeus was enraged by this and tasked his fellow Olympians to form the first woman out of clay and endow her with attributes designed to ruin men. Hephaestus formed her figure; Aphrodite gave her beauty; Athena clothed her and nurtured her 'feminine skills' like weaving and needlework; Hermes provided her with speech imbued with lies and a mind permeated with deceit; the goddesses Charites, Persuasion and the Horae (or hours) adorned her in jewels and a garland; Zeus gave her a jar containing 'countless plagues'. They dispatched her to Prometheus' brother Epimetheus as a bride. Pandora opened the jar and began to scatter its contents, releasing all its evils. Except hope. Pandora managed to shut the lid, preserving hope in spite of the atrocities enveloping humanity.

But why would hope be hidden in a jar of evils? There are possibly even more interpretations of this story than other myths, and it continues to puzzle readers and scholars alike. There are versions of the story that describe the jar as filled with blessings that are either bestowed on humanity or lost to humanity (sometimes due to a 'foolish man' letting them escape). The blessings version became popular with Renaissance artists and writers. The idea that Pandora had a box actually comes from an early modern mistake. Originally Pandora had a jar, but Erasmus, an influential sixteenth-century male scholar, mistranslated this and she's had a box ever since.

There are also varying interpretations of the popular version we know well. Was the inclusion of hope meant to be one comfort against all the evils released? Or, alternatively, was it held back from humanity in the box as punishment? Or have we mistranslated the Greek word *elpis* as 'hope' when it really meant 'deceptive expectation' or 'expectation of bad'? Unfortunately, there is no definitive answer, but Pandora's story is more valuable in terms of breaking down the misogyny embedded in it, considering she was custom-made to ruin lives. She is not the only 'first woman' to be made out of clay – male gods in other mythologies also created women from clay, including Hineahuone from Māori mythology. Her name literally means 'earth made woman' however she actually became a companion to her creator, rather than a tool for the destruction of humanity, suggesting that women had more equality and perhaps dealt with less misogyny in pre-colonial Māori culture than in the classical world.

Thematically, Pandora has a lot of similarities with Eve – both are blamed for the downfall of man in creation stories. Jane Harrison, feminist scholar and late nineteenth/early twentieth-century proponent for women's education, argued that early depictions show Pandora as the 'all-giving' earth mother. In this way she has been conflated with both Demeter and Gaia, with depictions of Pandora's birth showing her rising from the Earth itself. In contrast, according to Harrison's analysis, later depictions of Pandora show her as a death-and-destruction-causing mortal woman. Scholarship has moved on since then, but it is no surprise that feminist scholars are still deconstructing Pandora as both giver and destroyer. In film and television, Pandora's box frequently appears in popular culture without her, including *Lara Croft Tomb Raider: The Cradle of Life* and *The Librarians* franchise. However, Pandora is finally receiving some understanding in popular culture and even fashion – this author may or may not own a 'Justice for Pandora' T-shirt.

PASSIONATE PASIPHAË

Cretan queen Pasiphaë was technically a witch and sometimes known as the goddess of sorcery due to her divine parentage. Her father was the god Helios and her mother the ocean nymph Perse. She is most well-known for her failure at marriage and motherhood, and for her punishment by Poseidon for her husband's wrongdoing. King Minos of Crete had gained the throne with Poseidon's help, which meant that both Minos and Crete were always under Poseidon's thumb. Minos was required to sacrifice the finest bull to Poseidon each year, but one year there was a bull so stunning that he chose to sacrifice the second-best bull instead. Poseidon decided to punish Minos indirectly by inflicting Pasiphaë with a disturbing lust for the bull.

So that she could satisfy her desire, she begged Daedalus (architect, craftsman and father of Icarus) to construct a cow-shaped outer-shell that she could use to have sex with the bull. Her plan worked. She climbed inside a hollow wooden cow covered with hide, and the bull was able to impregnate her. The result was Asterion, more commonly known as the Minotaur, made famous from his labyrinth. Though we don't have the whole play, there are fragments from Euripides' play *Cretans* in which Pasiphaë defended herself to Minos, aware she was 'Suffering from some madness brought on by a god'. In the play, Euripides treats her as mortal, and she is sentenced to death by her husband (though her final outcome has not survived). Vergil portrays her as a dead mortal residing in the underworld in his *Aeneid*. In this story, she has been punished again in death and is relegated to the part of the underworld for unfulfilled and sinful lovers, known as the Fields of Mourning.

Her treatment by other Roman authors leans into the aspects of bestiality in her story to show the dangers of an uncontrolled woman, with Ovid even suggesting she took pleasure in her adultery with a bull. Her fall from divine being to a dirty zoophilic solidified her place amongst women ruled by their excessive sexuality in classical mythology, joining the ranks of women like Scylla and Phaedra, but whose actions were largely out of their control. Recent interpretations of Pasiphaë have followed suit and cast her as an antagonist, including Rick Riordan's novel *House of Hades* and Madeline Miller's highly acclaimed novel *Circe*. In Netflix's *KAOS*, Pasiphaë is a more complex character, neither good nor evil. She treated her daughter Ariadne badly but devotedly grieved the son she believed to be dead (but who was actually the Minotaur). Jennifer Saint asserts the feminist aspects of Pasiphaë's character in her 2021 novel *Ariadne*, particularly in her reaction to all she suffered at the hands of Minos and Poseidon.

LAMIA: A MOTHER'S GRIEF

In many ways, Lamia is difficult to categorise. Was she a homemaker, monster, madwoman, witch or femme fatale? She has been all five throughout her long history in literature and popular culture, but the defining feature of her life was the loss of her children and the inescapable grief she experienced as a mother. Her name translates to 'large shark' and in some stories she was seen as ghostly or serpentine. We don't know much about her story before her misfortunes began, besides her reputation as a beautiful Libyan queen. Zeus predictably fell for and impregnated her. Hera (also predictably) found out. From her ever-creative and cruel arsenal of punishments, Hera chose to deprive Lamia of her children, either by kidnapping and/or killing them or by making Lamia unwittingly kill them herself. Her loss drove her to utter despair. According to Late Antique sources, Hera also cursed Lamia with insomnia, so that she could never rest from her grieving. Zeus even gave Lamia the ability to remove her eyes, perhaps to try and help!? Unable to maintain her sanity, she succumbed to bloodlust and tried to console herself by murdering other mothers' children.

Her appearance mutated, turning her into a hideous, stinking monster on the outside, mirroring the pain and grief she felt inside. Sources from the first century CE onwards tend to portray Lamia as a seductress, feeding on the young men who were her conquests. Lamiae, a type of seductive phantom, spooked the ninth century Christian church and were identified as a potential threat to marriages. In colloquial Greek and Latin, women who threatened the status quo or lived outside the boundaries of acceptable femininity could be called Lamia as an insult – we see this occurring in stories involving witches and courtesans.

Lamia became something of a bogeywoman for ancient Greek children, and her name might be uttered by a mother or nursemaid as a warning to prevent children from misbehaving, for fear of her haunting or snatching them in the night. Lamia's impact was so strong that she even survives in modern Greek folklore, and she may be a precursor to modern vampire tales. She shares similarities with La Llorona in Mexican folklore, the wailing ghost of a woman who drowned her children and has mourned them ever since. La Llorona is also used to scare children and is said to cause death and tragedy to anyone who comes too near. Whilst both Lamia and La Llorona have been used as examples of unacceptable womanhood – specifically motherhood – La Llorona has enjoyed more of a recent feminist reinvention than Lamia. However, Lamia has fascinated horror, fantasy and science-fiction writers, appearing in various guises in movies and TV shows (including *Domino Day* and *Raised by Wolves*) and inspiring bands like Genesis and Iron Maiden.

From powerful mother goddesses like Gaia and Rhea, to the devoted wife Penelope and tragic figures like Lamia and Pasiphaë, these stories reflect the expectations and challenges of womanhood in ancient times. Modern interpretations and feminist reimaginings of mythological homemakers continue to resonate in contemporary culture, contributing to the ongoing dialogue about motherhood and gender roles. Although we might associate the term 'domestic goddess' with Nigella Lawson, it originally related to household goddesses. By 1847 it took on its contemporary meaning in Thackeray's *Vanity Fair*, referring to heroic female characters preferred by women compared to 'The kind, fresh, smiling, artless, tender little domestic goddess, whom men are inclined to worship.' Although much has thankfully changed for women since ancient times, many of the expectations to be a 'domestic goddess' not only remain but can also be harder to juggle with the increased pressure on women to 'have it all'. As Martha Stewart points out in her Netflix documentary, women like her were judged more harshly in the media not only because of their gender but also because they cultivated the perfect housewife image (until they didn't). Cultural critics have theorised that we are now in a 'retro domestic goddess moment,' but let's hope it's not that retro.

Virgin

Despite the immense pressure on women to marry and have children in the classical world, virgins were often revered in mythology. For ancient Greek women, virginity was often short-lived; a woman's primary function was to marry, run the household and produce children, duties she might fulfil as young as fourteen. In fact, it was considered medically dangerous to remain unmarried and childless. Goddesses, nymphs and other mythological women were shown to make their own rules and could live fulfilling lives as virgins. Artemis had her own clique of virginal nymphs, and her most devoted followers sometimes pledged celibacy to prove their loyalty.

Virgins played important roles in religious life, as priestesses of religious cults, central figures in religious festivals and in the form of several deities. Goddesses like Artemis, Athena and Hestia represented acceptable forms of divine virginity, as they could carry out their duties without distraction. Although they were powerful, or perhaps *because* they were powerful, they weren't considered appropriate role models for real ancient women due to their rejection of marriage and motherhood. In literature, they were often treated more like male gods, with a distinct separation between them and the mother goddesses. They would not hesitate to punish men for intruding on them (whereas many other women in mythology were at the mercy of men and their sexual desires) and have since become potent feminist symbols, particularly during the suffrage movement in the nineteenth and twentieth centuries.

WISE ATHENA

Athena is arguably the most important of the three virginal deities, especially in Athens, where she was patron goddess (hence the name). Athens was one of the foremost city-states of the ancient world, meaning Athena was one of the most important Olympian goddesses and appeared frequently in literature, especially as a protector of heroes like Odysseus. Ancient Greece was not a single unified country but a group of city-states, where a city and its surrounding area essentially acted as its own country, with its own laws and cultural practices. Sometimes these city-states even went to war against one another – like Athens and Sparta, who were longstanding enemies.

When Athens was created, Athena and Poseidon competed for patronage. Poseidon thrust his trident into the Acropolis and produced a spring of water, but it was undrinkable sea water – impressive but useless. Athena offered the people an olive tree, which was an essential crop in both ancient and modern Greece for its fruit, oil and timber. It was an easy choice for the Athenians. Poseidon was enraged by Athena's victory, marking the beginning of a longstanding feud between the two that frequently rears its head in stories of the heroes they protected, including the *Odyssey*. If you visit the Acropolis in Athens today, you can still see Athena's prominence in the city. Arguably the most famous Greek temple is the Parthenon, which dominates Athens' Acropolis with its sheer size and architectural detail. Dedicated to Athena, the name refers to Athena Parthenos (meaning Athena the Virgin) and her now-lost monumental statue, which almost reached the roof and was made of ivory and gold. There is also a sacred olive tree still standing in the spot where Athena conjured it, just outside the Erechtheion – the small temple decorated with caryatids (columns in the shape of women).

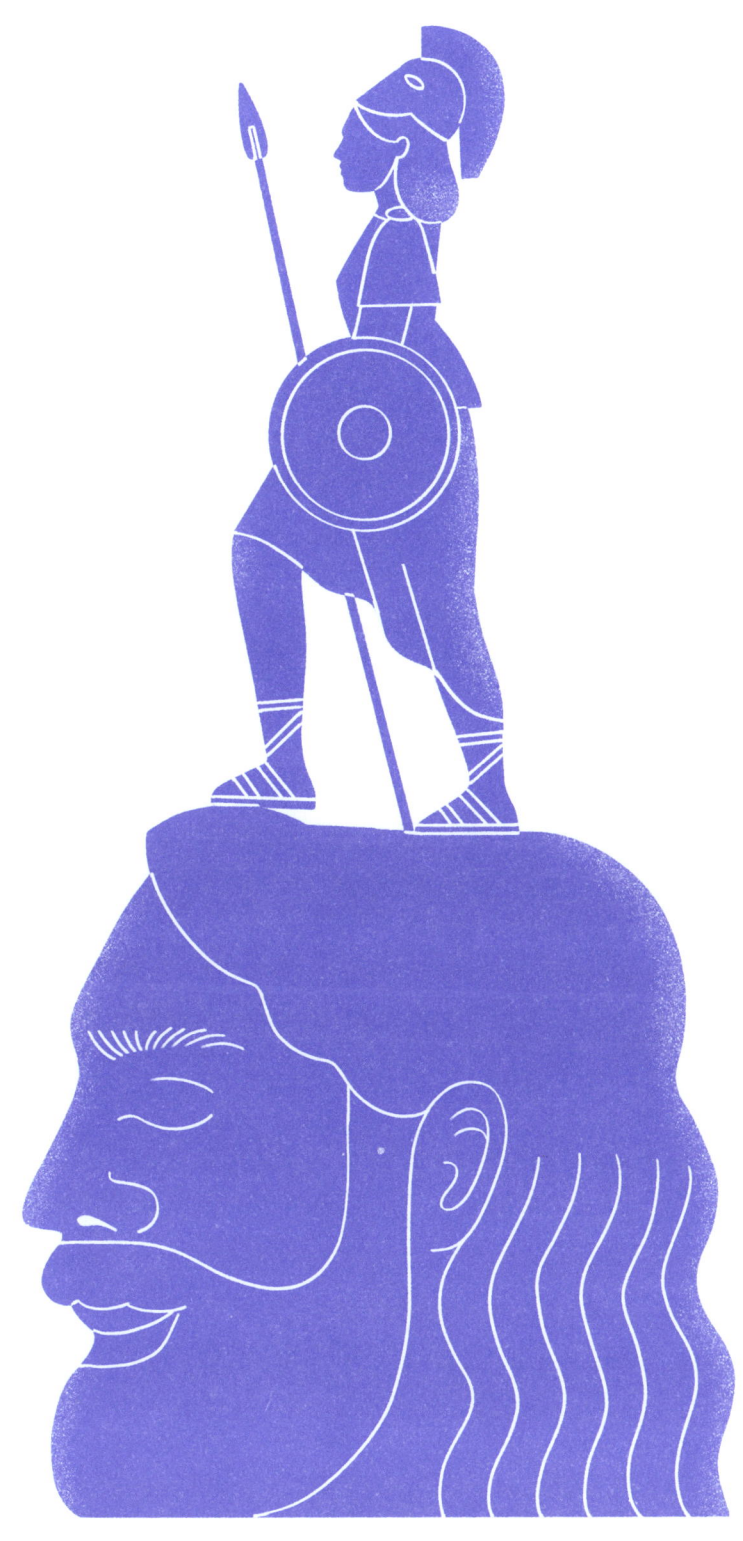

VIRGIN

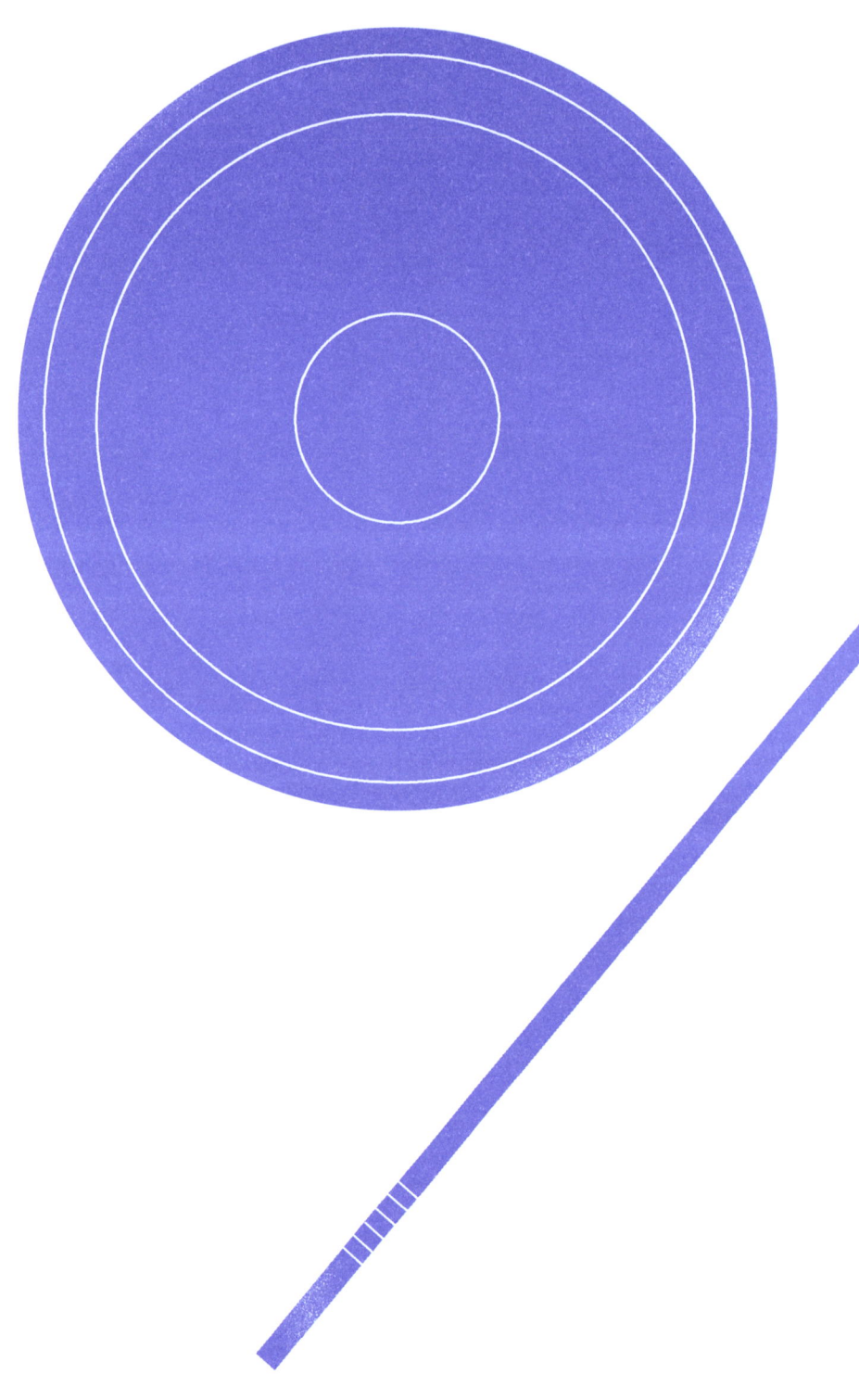

Athena has been used as a feminist symbol for centuries – in fact, some of our earliest feminist texts were inspired by Athena. In the prologue of one of her books about warfare, Christine de Pizan, a writer of the fourteenth-century French court, explains that she was able to write about masculine topics because of her connection to Minerva (the Roman name for Athena). The manuscript features a gorgeous illustration of Minerva watching over her as she writes.

Athena became particularly popular around the same time that women were fighting for both education and the vote in America, Britain and its colonies at the end of the nineteenth century and beginning of the twentieth. As the goddess of wisdom and crafts, she came to symbolise women's education, whilst her connection to defensive warfare and her masculine features emphasised her political potential. Her image was used on banners, flyers and on the cover of women's political magazines. She also appeared frequently as a character on stage in women's college dramatics. For the very same reasons, she was also used by those opposed to women's rights as a symbol of everything that was wrong with educated and feminist women, which the media labelled the 'New Woman'. There are many satirical cartoons depicting Athena as a 'New Woman', including in the famous *Punch* magazine, highlighting these modern women's so-called mannish features, including portrayals of them bicycle riding, smoking and reading. The 'New Woman's' knowledge of Classics, the ultimate elite and traditionally masculine subject, was also satirised with the image of Athena.

Whilst interpretations of Athena over the years are important to our understanding of her today, it would be a mistake to consider Athena a proto-feminist in the ancient world. We must remember that Athena didn't always have the greatest interactions with other women in ancient mythology. Some suggest that rather than being an ancient equivalent of a feminist, her strength and masculinity was used to perpetuate the patriarchy. As we will discover in later chapters, Athena had many female adversaries and doled out punishment to many women who didn't fit standard models of femininity, like Medusa. That doesn't mean feminist interpretations of Athena are any less valid. Like all the ancient goddesses, our understanding of her today is the culmination of many layers of analysis over thousands of years. The way Athena has been depicted in poetry and drama particularly reiterates the idea of her pride in her masculinity. She is often interpreted as butch, and has become a bit of a sapphic icon over the last century.

Freud, the most famous psychoanalyst, had a statuette of Athena on his desk, which he used as a therapeutic prop for patients to make their own observations as well as a visual aid to help explain his contentious theories of 'penis envy' and the 'castration complex'. He believed that the disembodied Gorgon head (the type of monster Medusa was) on Athena's breastplate made her sexually unapproachable because he associated the decapitated head with male castration. He related it to the 'castration complex' that he believed women felt due to their lack of penis, more commonly known as penis envy. He went even further to theorise that Athena was frightening to men because of the strong male homosexual culture of ancient Greece. He tried to convince his patient, the queer modernist poet H.D., that the statuette's 'lack of a spear' represented 'penis envy'. However, H.D. later insisted that 'woman is perfect' and used the statuette to discuss her bisexuality and the fact that she felt she had both masculine and feminine qualities. H.D.'s lifelong companion was the English writer Bryher and the two women often used classical mythology in their work and correspondence with one another.

Athena's own relationship with women is complex. Despite her feminist status today, she didn't appear to have any particular empathy for women, mortal or otherwise, except for fellow virgins. As Ovid recounts, when Poseidon tried to rape the mortal maiden Corone (Greek for crow) and nobody answered her cries for help, Athena took pity on her as a virgin and transformed her into a crow so she could escape. However, she was possibly more passionate about punishing her enemies than fostering female friendships. At one point she became enamoured with another mortal maiden, Myrmex (spoiler alert: her name is Greek for ant), who was renowned for her chastity and intelligence. In fact, Athena loved her so much that scholars now debate whether the language used in the story gives lesbian vibes. Athena happened to invent the plough during their companionship, but Myrmex betrayed her by stealing the credit, breaking Athena's heart. The obvious solution was to turn Myrmex into an ant.

In some stories, Athena was so far removed from female relationships that she had no mother at all and was born from Zeus alone. However, the more popular version is that Athena sprang from her father Zeus' head after he swallowed her pregnant mother Metis whole. Metis was Zeus' first wife and was instrumental in his victory against the Titans, but she was unable to escape Zeus' paranoia after it was prophesied that his son would be more powerful than him and his daughter wiser than her mother. That daughter turned out to be Athena. Metis gave birth to Athena inside Zeus' head and helped her to escape by crafting her armour and weaponry, which Athena clanged together until Zeus' headache became so unbearable that he had to have his head cut open. Out sprang Athena, fully grown and armed.

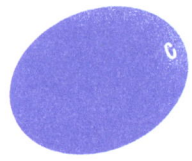

Despite her mother's dedication and her father's attempt to kill her, Athena didn't hold it against him. In some texts, she seems to reject her mother altogether, and in doing so diminishes motherhood in general. During the 1920s, Classicist Jane Harrison described it as 'A desperate theological expedient to rid an Earth-born Kore [maiden] of her matriarchal conditions.' The playwright Aeschylus has Athena making the final judgement on Orestes after he killed his mother Clytemnestra, whose lover had killed her husband. In his play *Eumenides*, Athena votes for Orestes, exclaiming: 'For there was no mother who gave me birth; and in all things, except for marriage, wholeheartedly I am for the male and entirely on the father's side.'

VIRGIN

ARTEMIS AND HER ENTOURAGE

Artemis could not have been more different from Athena in her attitude towards other women, although the two are often grouped together as virgin Olympian goddesses who didn't follow traditional gender norms. Artemis had close relationships with several female mythological characters, and her story is open to many contemporary queer interpretations. Many stories about Artemis feature a sisterhood of followers, usually nymphs. She is now better known as the goddess of the hunt, wilderness, nature and the moon (through her later conflation with the moon goddess Selene) – she even lends her name to NASA's current moon exploration project. Artemis was also a protector of young girls and did not hesitate to punish men who threatened their privacy and chastity. Her Roman counterpart was Diana, which might be her most familiar moniker today.

Perhaps the most famous (and violent) story of Artemis involves the male hunter Actaeon, who came from a well-known mythological family. The specific nature of Actaeon's transgression varies, but in all the stories his punishment is the same – Artemis turns him into a stag and has his hunting dogs maul and eat him. Some of the most famous writers of the classical world were inspired to create their own versions of the story, including Euripides, Aeschylus, Callimachus, Hesiod and Ovid. In ancient vase paintings, Artemis often has an ally in the minor goddess Lyssa, who is depicted infecting Actaeon's dogs with rabies (she was a spirit of the disease), as well as rage and fury. The poet Callimachus offered the most recognised reason for Artemis' vengeance in describing Actaeon spying on a nude Artemis bathing. But other versions of the story exist, including Actaeon committing hubris by boasting that he was a superior hunter to Artemis or even more shockingly, wanting to marry Artemis herself. Today we might interpret Artemis' revenge as feminist rage, but the story was originally a warning about the harm women could do if they had access to power, as well as a lesson to mortals about messing with the gods.

Although some of the other goddesses had their own female followers, nothing compares to Artemis' loyal entourage of both nymphs and mortal maidens. Callisto, whose name comes from the word for 'most beautiful', was the most famous of Artemis' followers. In some stories Callisto was a nymph and in others she was the daughter of a mythological king. She swore herself and her chastity to Artemis, but Zeus decided that he liked the look of her, as he did with many innocent maidens. When unexpectedly separated from her female companions whilst out hunting, Callisto was seduced by Artemis. Unfortunately, 'Artemis' turned out to be Zeus in disguise, ready to commit another rape. Callisto fell pregnant and, even though it was not her fault, was expelled from Artemis' entourage and turned into a bear by Hera (though in later versions of the story it was Artemis). Hesiod described a comic version (now lost) in which the sapphic element of the story was ramped up and Callisto even blamed Artemis for impregnating her. This clearly pissed Artemis off, so she transformed Callisto into a bear. Years later, the son Callisto bore became a hunter and almost killed her, before Zeus turned her into the constellation we know today as Ursa Major (meaning 'Great Bear'). More recently, this story has been interpreted as lesbian or queer, inspiring many lesbian authors and artists, presumably encouraged by the numerous artworks produced over the centuries portraying Zeus as Artemis seducing Callisto.

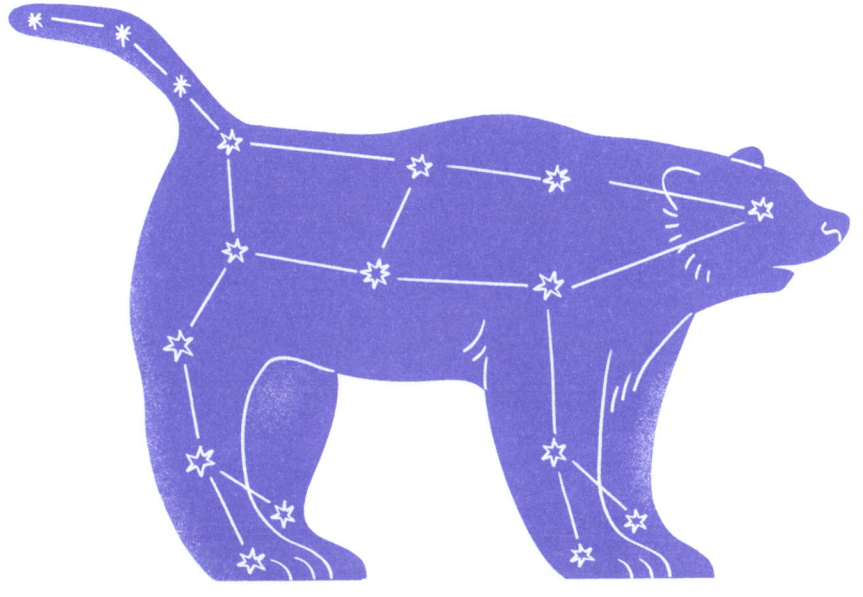

Besides Callisto, the bulk of Artemis' followers comprised 20 Amnisiades, river nymphs from Amnisos in Crete, and 60 Oceanides, part of a group of 3,000 sea nymphs born to Titans. Artemis also borrowed the muses from her brother Apollo on occasion and fellow goddess Persephone even counted herself as one of Artemis' followers, causing Artemis to appear frequently in literature about the ever-popular Hades–Persephone–Demeter myth. She is also one of the most popular deities with mortals and traces of her can be found in contemporary literature, especially Young Adult Speculative Fiction and Fantasy. Even if she is not specifically named, you can find Artemis in characters like Katniss Everdeen in *The Hunger Games*, highlighting that Artemis was, and always will be, a role model to young women.

VIRGIN

HESTIA THE HOMEBODY

The first child of the Titans Rhea and Cronos, Hestia was the goddess of home and hearth (the fireplace used for heating and cooking, and the essential focal point of the ancient household). She was eaten by her father and saved by her mother Rhea and brother Zeus (see page 33). Sadly, we don't have as many stories about Hestia from ancient writers, but she was an essential part of everyday life in ancient Greece and Rome. Her sanctuary was the primary hearth of each city, town or village, located in the government buildings known as a *prytaneion*. Like her nieces, Athena and Artemis, Hestia purposefully chose not to marry and to remain an eternal virgin. Both Poseidon (her brother) and Apollo (her nephew) asked for her hand in marriage, prompting her to declare an oath of chastity before Zeus.

In Rome, she was known as Vesta and had a group of six real-life priestesses known as the Vestal Virgins. These girls were chosen as youngsters by the high priest of Rome (who happened to also be the emperor) and were expected to remain chaste and serve for at least thirty years. They had to ensure that one of them was always guarding the sacred hearth, otherwise they would be whipped as punishment. If they broke their vow of chastity, they would be buried alive and their lover publicly beaten to death. However, despite these strict rules, being a Vestal Virgin was a high honour with great social status, allowing privileges unavailable to the masses and a generous pension upon retirement. They could marry after their service was completed, though this was rare, and some even chose to renew their vows of chastity to Vesta. It is likely that Hestia also had priestesses as part of her cult, but their status was less prominent than their Roman counterparts as we have almost no surviving sources about them. Because of the very strict requirements for being an Athenian citizen (and therefore being allowed to participate in politics), marriage was more valuable for women than religious vows of chastity in Greece. Whereas in Rome, women could be citizens (though couldn't vote) and they could enjoy more financial freedom.

Hestia herself was free from many of the gods' petty feuds, largely due to her lack of interest in love and sex as well as her need to stay close to the fires of home. When other gods were away in battle, Hestia protected their hearth, and as a result she is often missing from many of the large sculptural scenes of the gods commonly adorning temples, such as the Gigantomachy (a battle between the Olympian gods and a race of giants). In one of the earliest surviving written sources relating to Hestia, the *Homeric Hymn to Aphrodite* (composed sometime between the seventh and fifth centuries BCE), Aphrodite is said to have no power over Hestia. Since Aphrodite is usually able to influence other deities, this indicates how powerful Hestia really was, despite being often overlooked due to her domestic nature as so many women in both mythology and history have been over the years.

Like a Virgin

These three virgin goddesses are arguably the most prominent in Western culture, besides the Virgin Mary, of course. Mary does have connections to virgin characters in both Arthurian and Slavic mythology. Zorya was the virgin Slavic personification (and possibly goddess) of dawn. She was the daughter of the sun god, Dazhbog, and opened the gates to his palace every morning and took care of his horses. In Lithuanian versions of the myth, she is the Morning Star and, along with her sister the Evening Star, is a daughter of the female sun deity. They also appear in Russian mythology as the two virgin sisters, Zorya Utrennyaya (goddess of dawn) and Zorya Vechernyaya (goddess of dusk), living on the mythical island of Buyan. In Slovenian narrative folk song tradition, Dawn and Dusk are rivals. Dawn appears frequently in Ukrainian folk music too, particularly in wedding songs.

Dawn is invoked in prayers and incantations, especially to cure sickness. Over time, the two figures have assimilated and are used interchangeably in verbal folk magic (known as *zagovory*). Mary eventually replaced Dawn in East Slavic charms after a period of transition when they appear as the same person – 'Maria the Dawn'. Similarly, there are Virgin Mary-adjacent figures in Arthurian legend, particularly in Geoffrey of Monmouth's *Life of Merlin*, in which Morgen (a version of Morgan le Fay) is a virginal good witch who uses her powers for the benefit of others. She could fly and used her special skills in mathematics and astronomy to teach her fellow-virgin sisters. These sisters might also relate to a possible real-life group of nine virgin priestesses reported by the Roman geographer Pomponius Mela, thought to have healing powers by the Gauls.

Either way, there is a clear connection between virginity and the power to do good within pagan traditions, which was later adopted by the Christian church. Lourdes is famous as a Christian pilgrimage site, where the Virgin Mary supposedly first appeared to a teenage girl in the mid-nineteenth century. Since then, they claim over 7,000 cases of healing, 70 of which have been miracles recognised by the church – there is even a medical bureau dedicated to sorting and recording these claims. Over 80% of the 'miracles' are attributed to women.

Today we have a complex relationship to the idea of virginity, with young women seemingly never able to win. During young adolescence and early adulthood, you might be considered a prude for not losing your virginity early enough and a slut for losing it too early. The Madonna-Whore complex describes this trap, and the men who can only view women as either one or the other. Outside of the Christian church and other major religions that teach chastity until marriage, the idea of virginity is largely fetishised – the notion of a man 'taking' a girl's virginity has become a disturbing trope relating to control and possession. However, when we look beyond the surface, the concept of female virginity within the church and classical traditions has essentially served the same purpose from the beginning: to ensure 'legitimate' children and as a culturally accepted excuse to oppress women's bodies.

Warrior

Warrior women were not always seen as the heroines they are today. When we think of women warriors from the ancient world, the Amazons are easily the most celebrated and iconic. However, the Amazons were originally created by the Greeks as a symbol of everything uncivilised, a reputation that lasted for thousands of years – even as women activists began to reclaim the term 'Amazon' for themselves, it was still used as an insult in the nineteenth and twentieth centuries. Ironically, the attributes designed to situate the Amazons as the antithesis of a civilised woman and of Greek culture itself are often the very attributes that many women are drawn to as inspiration today, like their expression of female masculinity and ability to face men in combat. There were, of course, always exceptions. Atalanta was one of the only mortal heroines of Greek mythology who received positive treatment and led the way for figures such as Joan of Arc in popular culture. Warrior-types from other cultures often get erroneously conflated with Amazons, but they all served their own unique functions within their respective mythologies, telling us a lot about how women were viewed in ancient cultures across the world.

AMAZONS

The Amazons lived and trained together in isolation and were known for their skills in archery. One of the most memorable tales of the Amazons is that they cut off one breast to more easily use a bow and arrow. Their name possibly means 'breastless', but there are other theories, including 'husbandless'. Homer refers to them in the *Iliad* as the equals of men. To the Greeks they represented the undesirable and barbaric 'other', often standing in for 'the enemy' in Greek architectural features and works of art. In the origin myth of Athens, the Amazons almost conquered the Athenians in the Attic War, but were ultimately defeated thanks to the Greek hero Theseus, who ended up falling for the Amazonian queen, Hippolyta. Hippolyta was the daughter of Otrera (first queen of the Amazons) and Ares (god of war), and in the historian Plutarch's interpretation of events, Hippolyta was the one to end the war with a peace treaty and subsequent marriage to Theseus. However, alternate versions suggest that Theseus dumped Hippolyta for Phaedra, who ultimately fell for Theseus and Hippolyta's son, Hippolytus, thanks to Aphrodite's meddling (page 118).

In order to continue their all-female society, the Amazons did have to reproduce with men, but they returned any sons to their fathers and proudly raised their daughters as future warriors. They supposedly lived in what is now Turkey and had their own capital, Themiscyra, beside the Thermodon river. The Greek heroes Heracles, Theseus and Jason all made expeditions to the city. In DC's comic and movie franchise *Wonder Woman*, Themiscyra (called Paradise Island from 1941 until 1987) is depicted as an island nation city-state governed by Aphrodite's Law, which promised immortality if no man ever set foot on the island. From the nineties onwards, *Wonder Woman* comics have made reference to Themiscyra as a sapphic paradise and to Wonder Woman's possible bisexuality. There is some archaeological evidence for women warriors in the Eurasian Steppes, particularly in modern-day Ukraine and Russia, but whether these are remnants of the mythological Amazons is unknown.

Amazonian society was ruled by a queen, the most famous of which were Hippolyta and her sister Penthesilea, who became queen on her death. They had two other sisters, Melanippe and Antiope, who betrayed the others and eventually married the hero Theseus. They were the daughters of Ares, god of war, and Otrera, the mythological founder of the Amazons. It was believed that Otrera also founded the Temple of Artemis at Ephesus, which was a particularly significant shrine, as the Amazons were said to worship Artemis. Callimachus detailed this story in his *Hymn to Artemis*. Historically, the temple offered sanctuary to those in danger of persecution or punishment, and there are tales of the Amazons seeking safety there from both Heracles and Dionysus.

Penthesilea accidentally killed her sister, either in battle or a hunting accident (there are different versions of the myth), and serving as queen did not sit easily with her. Unlike many other tragic heroines of Greek mythology, she was a warrior, and so she devised a plan to die in battle. She reigned during the Trojan War and attempted to support the Trojans, who were from the same region (now Turkey). She led an army of Amazons to Troy, but arrived late to the battle. After distinguishing herself in battle, she was famously killed by Achilles, who supposedly fell in love with her corpse. These events took place just after the ending of Homer's *Iliad*, but the original story, from the epic poem *Aethiopis*, has been lost. However, the Roman author Vergil also tells her story in his *Aeneid*, which details the mythological founding of Rome by defeated Trojan royalty. Since the Amazons were on the same side as Rome's fabled Trojan ancestors, Vergil portrays Penthesilea quite favourably before her tragic end: 'The ferocious Penthesilea, gold belt fastened beneath her exposed breast, leads her battle-lines of Amazons with their crescent light-shields ... a warrioress, a maiden who dares to fight with men.' This female warrior (or *bellatrix* in Latin) absolutely proved her worth in battle against the Greeks, and the Amazons were close to victory. But the outcome of the Trojan War was inevitable, especially since the stories we have were told by Greeks rather than Amazons or Trojans. According to Diodorus, the Trojan War marked the end of Amazonian glory and their exploits were eventually seen as legend and not fact.

The Amazons also made their way to Roman Italy – in literature and supposedly in person – and inspired new characters. When Penthesilea failed to return from the Trojan War, her young maid Clete led a search party, but they were ravaged by storms and shipwrecked on the toe of Italy's boot. They settled in the region, naming it Clete after their new leader. These Italian Amazons likely inspired Vergil's Camilla, a warrior woman from a tribe bordering Rome who fought against Aeneas, echoing the battle of Achilles and Penthesilea. Female warriors were certainly not unheard of in Rome. There were multiple accounts of women in battle, and even whilst Vergil was composing the *Aeneid*, a Nubian warrior-queen named Amanirenas defeated Augustus' Roman troops. It was also common for Roman generals and emperors to claim they had defeated Amazons in battle, with Aurelian and Pompey both showing off so-called 'Amazons' in victory parades. Aurelian's group comprised women dressed in masculine attire caught amongst the Goths, and Pompey's were likely Scythian women.

The playwright Aeschylus described the Amazons as 'the unwed, flesh-devouring Amazons' and negative connotations surrounding them continued until the twentieth century. The name was used as a slur against suffragettes, lesbians and gender-nonconforming people until queer women began to reclaim it. At the beginning of the twentieth century, the Women's Social and Political Union (aka the suffragettes) formed a secret society called 'The Bodyguard' unit, consisting of up to thirty women. They trained in Jujitsu and provided security for suffragette leaders at rallies and other events. The suffragettes soon became known colloquially and in the media as Amazons, with the title once again being used against women who represented 'unacceptable womanhood' in the same way that they did in ancient Greece. When the male-only University of Oxford began opening women's colleges in the late twentieth century, men complained about the 'invasion of the Amazons'.

The term became popular for lesbians in early twentieth-century France, including the infamous Natalie Clifford Barney and her circle of queer women, the so-called 'Lesbos-on-Seine' in Paris. The bisexual artist Marie Laurencin created several sketches and paintings on the theme 'Amazon', featuring Natalie as muse and model. One of the key historical women featured in Judy Chicago's feminist masterpiece *The Dinner Party*, Barney was nicknamed the Amazon because she made headlines by riding horses astride instead of side-saddle like a 'proper' lady. *The Dinner Party* also featured a place setting for an Amazon (meant to represent all Amazons), with some of their individual names inscribed on the floor. The Amazon plate is decorated with breasts covered in silver and gold, referring to their breastplates worn in battle.

The popularity of the Amazons blossomed in the 1970s and 1980s, with many groups and publications taking inspiration from this mythical community of women, including New Zealand's lesbian softball team 'The Amazons', founded in 1977. In *Buffy the Vampire Slayer*, the lesbian witches Willow and Tara reassure each other that they can be 'Strong like an Amazon.' Aside from the whole living in a women-only society thing, it is the Amazons' strength and brazen defiance of gender norms that inspire feminists and queer people today.

SRIKANDI

Ancient warrior women have become queer idols in many cultures. Srikandi/Shikhandi was an ancient warrior princess from the Hindu epic *Mahabharata*. As a warrior, Srikandi was in a very public position as a soldier, she was skilled at archery, resilient in battle and unafraid to face the most fearsome opponents. She was known for her courage, ability to speak up for herself and self-confidence. Srikandi's name is frequently invoked in discussions around women's rights in Indonesia and she is seen as a feminist superhero.

In Hindu versions of the tale Shikhandi was born female but agreed to change their gender to male after an encounter with a nature spirit known as a Yaksha. In some Indonesian traditions, particularly in wayang (shadow puppetry), Srikandi was born and/or raised male and became female, going on to marry the warrior Arjuna. Many LGBTQ+ people cannot live openly in Indonesia today, but some look towards familiar mythological figures, like Srikandi, as role models. Srikandi has especially become something of an icon for Indonesian trans women. *Children of Srikandi* (2012), the first film of its kind, features traditional shadow puppetry alongside documentary footage to tell the story of trans and queer women in Indonesia.

ATALANTA

Atalanta was supposed to be a boy. At least, she was according to her father. He ordered her to be exposed, a tragic historical practice of killing an unwanted baby by leaving it in the wild to starve, be eaten by animals, die of hypothermia or even be taken by slave traders. Atalanta was found by a female bear whose cubs had just been killed. She nursed Atalanta until a group of hunters discovered her and raised her in the mountains. She-bears were associated with Artemis, to whom Atalanta devoted herself for life. She copied Artemis' typical dress of a knee-length sleeveless tunic and lived in the wilderness. Like her patron goddess, Atalanta also committed herself to chastity, though not without danger. With her archery skills, she famously killed two centaurs who attempted to rape her. Her name derives from the Greek word meaning 'equal in weight', potentially referring to her equal footing with men.

Atalanta is sometimes called the Greek Amazon, and though she competed with men as their equal, she did not necessarily threaten patriarchal Greek civilisation in the same way as the Amazons and often aided Greek heroes. In some versions of *Jason and the Argonauts*, Atalanta joined as the only woman in their party as they searched for the golden fleece. Medea (Jason's witchy wife) healed Atalanta when she was wounded in battle. Her notable feats also include beating Achilles' father, Peleus, in a wrestling match, which was a popular subject for vase decoration. When a gigantic and savage boar terrorised Calydon, the king called for heroes to slay the beast. Atalanta answered and beat the men to draw first blood, winning the boarskin as her prize. The Calydonian boar hunt had an unexpected outcome: Atalanta's father recognised her as his daughter, so (for some reason) she reunited with him, and he immediately started pressuring her to get married, as all 'good' girls should. Trying to stop these marriage arrangements, Atalanta insisted that any potential suitor must beat her in a footrace, which she confidently knew was impossible. She insisted that any suitor who lost be killed on the spot, hoping this would prevent any man from even trying. It would have worked out swimmingly had Aphrodite not gotten involved and helped a suitor named Hippomenes cheat in the race. Tragically, Atalanta was forced to marry him. Tragically, Atalanta was forced to marry him and it was not a happy ending (page. 118).

During the late nineteenth century, she loaned her name to a British girls' magazine founded by L.T. Meade, a very popular feminist novelist whose stories were aimed at girls and young women. She helped to create the college girl and girls' boarding school genre of novels, which is still popular today. *Atalanta* offered girls opportunities to better themselves through awards for submitted essays and also promoted women's higher education. In 1920 a woman's football team named after Atalanta was founded in West Yorkshire by the region's first female reporter, Constance Waller, who was dubbed an 'advanced feminist' at the time. Olympic javelin-thrower Fatima Whitbread, who won Gold for Britain in 1987, even said that she was inspired to train in athletics because of the myth of Atalanta. Emily Hauser's 2017 novel *For the Winner* tells the story of Jason and the Argonauts from Atalanta's perspective, giving a voice to the one woman allowed to go on the quest of a lifetime with a company of men. In the 2023 novel *Atalanta*, Jennifer Saint fleshed out her relationship with Medea and highlights Atalanta's disappointment that Medea chooses to shrink herself into the role of Jason's wife. Saint's novel critiques the cruel, predatory nature of men in Greek mythology and history and recognises Atalanta as a feminist heroine navigating the patriarchy in many ways that mirror contemporary society.

JOAN OF ARC

Although a real historical figure, Joan of Arc (c.1412– 1431) is shrouded by mythologies and is a personal patron saint and icon to many. Even prior to canonisation in 1920, Joan was a popular symbol, with many examples of antique Joan of Arc amulets that people carried to inspire confidence. Heretic, martyr, witch, feminist, lesbian, cross-dresser, intersex, transgender, asexual, schizophrenic – these are all labels that have been applied to Joan of Arc and may have contributed to Joan losing the infamous heresy trial and ultimately burning at the stake, which was engineered by the British to shame the French. In fact, it was the offense of 'cross-dressing' that qualified Joan for the death penalty, as it counted as a second offense of heresy. Although we may never know the truth, Joan's role as a modern LGBTIQ+ legend has been solidified, providing inspiration for many writers and artists, including Vita Sackville-West, who published a very queer biography in 1936 entitled *Saint Joan of Arc*. In 2022, Joan made a triumphant appearance on The Globe Stage as a non-binary warrior in the play *I, Joan* by non-binary playwright Charlie Josephine. They drew attention to the fact that the queer community needs stories like Joan's, even if the line between history and mythology is blurred, because so much queer history been erased.

VALKYRIES

Valkyries are often compared with Amazons, particularly because of their depictions in modern media. In recent years, both have featured in blockbusters based on comics, with Valkyries appearing in the *Marvel Cinematic Universe* (usually alongside Thor). However, the Valkyries' function within their own culture's mythology was completely different based on their frequent descriptions in thirteenth- and fourteenth-century Norse poetry. Whilst the Amazons were barbaric warriors and enemies to civilised society, Valkyries played a vital role for Norse warriors: they entered the battlefield to select warriors who would die in battle and be allowed to enter Valhalla, the hall of heroes in the afterlife. They also served mead to the newly recruited dead warriors, so a lot of early depictions of Valkyries show them as cup-bearers. Although they were armed with spears and shielded by helmets and chainmail to survive the battlefield, they were not meant to be warriors themselves. Whilst the Marvel Valkyries are equipped with swords known as Dragonfang, they were almost never depicted with swords in the art or literature of Norse mythology because swords were strictly masculine tools. Valkyries emboldened and consoled men going into battle with the promise of an ideal afterlife in Valhalla. There is no archaeological evidence to show that women regularly trained as warriors during the Viking age, but the legend of the Valkyrie as a figure of the male imagination took hold and has since become part of popular culture.

SEKHMET

One of the key goddesses in the ancient Egyptian pantheon was Sekhmet, a lion-headed goddess of war and a seeker of vengeance against Ra's enemies. Her name literally meant 'she who is powerful', and she was both a bringer and healer of disease. She breathed fire and had an insatiable bloodlust that almost destroyed the world, but her fellow deities tricked her into drinking a large quantity of dyed-red beer, thinking it was blood. In her drunkenness, she chose peace and returned home. To commemorate this near-apocalyptic event, Egyptians held a yearly festival of intoxication, where there is archaeological evidence of Sekhmet's priestesses overindulging. We can tell that she was an extremely important figure in Egyptian religion and society, as well as to collectors of Egyptian antiquities, because there are more representations of Sekhmet in museums and collections than any other Egyptian god or goddess. She also became a popular figure amongst feminists, particularly during the nineteenth- and twentieth-century Egyptomania, which coincided with the discovery of significant archaeological finds as well as women carving out their place within the field of archaeology. Sekhmet became a popular motif in Egyptian revival jewellery during the 1920s – Cartier even created a stunning brooch featuring an original Egyptian faience portrait of Sekhmet in 1923, which sold for over a million US dollars at auction in 2013. Today, Sekhmet is more commonly associated with new-age movements, such as neopaganism and goddess spirituality.

Because warrior women did not represent acceptable womanhood and were often othered, women and gender nonconforming people who do not meet society's expectations have derived strength from their legendary tales. Newer interpretations of warrior women have influenced our understanding of them today, but what is mythology if not a layering of stories and meanings over centuries?

Femme
Fatale

Despite multiple tales of rape, largely perpetrated by the gods, a woman was often blamed for a man's assault or mistreatment of her. In fact, seduction had a more severe punishment than rape and was a more serious crime for the woman's family. Seduction could be punished by death, whereas rape was barely considered a crime and was rarely prosecuted. In Homer's *Odyssey*, Calypso was blamed for keeping Odysseus captive for seven years on her island, personifying the connection between Eros and pride. Even Helen of Troy, who was kidnapped for her beauty, was blamed for the Trojan War. Her sister, Clytemnestra, was also portrayed as the ultimate anti-wife – she had an affair whilst her husband was at war (contrasting with the ever-faithful Penelope) and murdered him upon his return. Although the label 'femme fatale' might suggest eroticism and power, most of these tales end in tragedy for the women involved – included in order to reflect ancient Greek values about women and their position in society. Today, the femme fatale figure is given a more positive spin, in that the women hold the power, which these victimised women from ancient mythology lacked.

APHRODITE: A THIN LINE BETWEEN LOVE AND HATE

Born from Uranus' castrated genitalia, which his son had hurled into the ocean, Aphrodite had no mother. But that did not stop her from becoming the original femme fatale. She was the goddess of love, beauty, procreation and pleasure, but she wasn't all sunshine and roses. Although she was married to Hephaestus (a disabled god known for his kindness and ingenuity, but not his physique), she had affairs with other gods such as Poseidon, Dionysus, Hermes and especially Ares, god of war. She played a central role in the Trojan War, described in the *Iliad*, and in the events that followed, described in the Roman epic poem the *Aeneid*. It could be said that she even started the war in the first place, by promising to give Helen to Paris so that he would vote her the most beautiful in a contest amongst the goddesses Athena and Hera. She also happens to seduce a Trojan prince named Anchises and birthed a certain Trojan/Roman hero named Aeneas, who stars in Vergil's *Aeneid* and is Rome's answer to Odysseus. She intervenes on his behalf on the battlefield and beyond. But she also had a habit of punishing those who didn't worship her sufficiently, as well as manipulating mortals and even other gods with her charms.

Hippolytus, son of the king of Athens, denounced not only Aphrodite but love itself. He worshipped Artemis, above all, who valued chastity and everything Aphrodite despised. She devised an elaborate revenge plan, making Hippolytus' stepmother, Phaedra, obsessed with him. When she tried to seduce him, he rejected her with disgust, prompting the addled Phaedra to claim to her husband that Hippolytus had raped her. Hippolytus' father believed his wife over his son and implored the god Poseidon (who happened to be his father in some stories) to punish him. Poseidon provoked Hippolytus' horses to trample him to death, in turn causing Phaedra to take her own life.

In another tale of punishment for ungratefulness, Aphrodite arranged a tragic end for Atalanta and Hippomenes, whose marriage she manipulated in the first place. Hippomenes had fallen in love with Atalanta, a huntress and princess who vowed never to marry. To avert pressure from her father, she proclaimed she would only marry a man who could outrun her. Under normal circumstances, Hippomenes could never have beaten her, but Aphrodite provided him with golden apples to distract Atalanta, which worked (for some reason) and allowed him to win, resulting in their marriage. However, he was foolish enough not to thank Aphrodite, therefore she compelled Hippomenes and Atalanta to commit sacrilege by having sex at a sanctuary, which pissed off the other gods. In retaliation, either Zeus, Cybele, Rhea or Artemis (who was particularly upset at Atalanta losing her virginity) turned them into lions, believing that lions could not mate with one another. In these tales, poor Phaedra and Atalanta were caught in the crosshairs of Aphrodite's wrath against the men who didn't satisfy her, as women in Greek mythology so often were.

FEMME FATALE

Like so many other female characters throughout history, Aphrodite is often at odds with other women or in competition with them, usually with a man at the centre. She cursed fellow goddess Eos (the dawn) with an insatiable desire for young mortal men because she slept with her extramarital lover, Ares. In cahoots with Hera (also infamously vindictive), she forced Medea to fall in love with Jason so she could use her skills in sorcery to help him take possession of the golden fleece. But Medea's unnatural love for Jason ultimately drove her to madness and infanticide. On another occasion, Aphrodite was eclipsed by a mere mortal princess named Psyche (the origin of the word we use today), who was compared to Aphrodite in beauty, and who other mortals even began worshipping. She enlisted her son Eros to help her take revenge, ordering him to pierce Psyche with one of his arrows and make her fall in love with a hideous beast. However, he accidentally nicked himself with his own arrow and fell for her instead. As a result, she tortured Psyche and set her on a series of impossible trials, but the other gods intervened and help Psyche succeed.

Aphrodite/Venus has always been a major figure in pop culture, but she is primarily celebrated today for her sexual freedom rather than her wrathful side. She's inspired artists for millennia and allowed them to push boundaries regarding nude representation. She's lent her name to countless pop songs, including Lady Gaga's 2013 single 'Venus' inspired by the goddess Venus, the planet Venus and sex. She is also an important figure in Wicca and neopaganism. Aphrodite is a much more complicated persona than contemporary media representations allow, but she would be delighted to know that she is still worshipped.

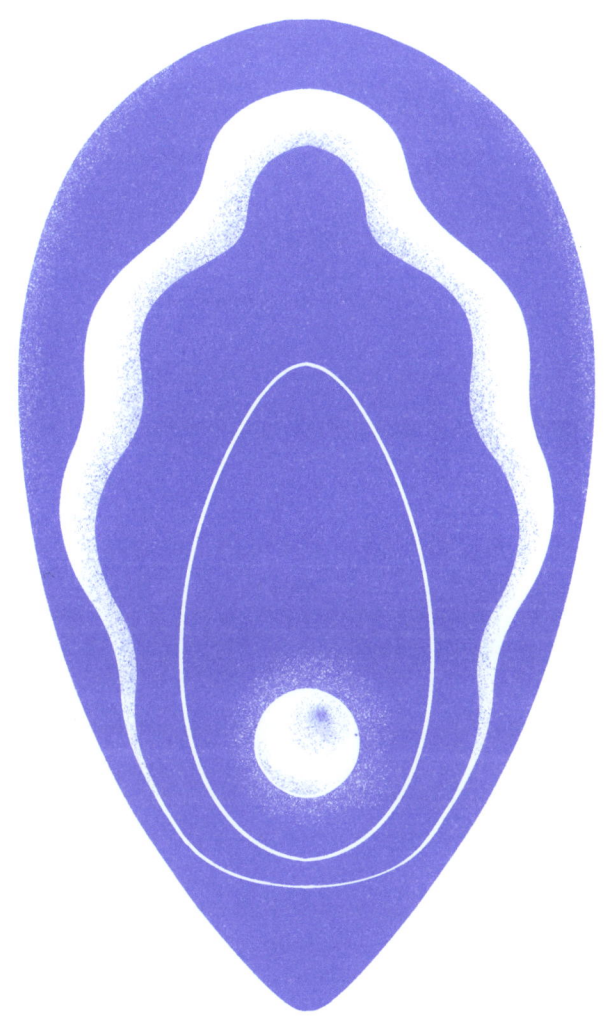

HELEN OF TROY: THE FACE THAT LAUNCHED A THOUSAND SHIPS

Helen is quite a controversial figure in Greek mythology. We know her today as a famed beauty and 'the face that launched a thousand ships', but how much control did she have over her own fate? Let's begin with her conception, where the theme of sexual violence in Helen's life first emerged when Zeus raped her mother Leda. Helen's conception has been imomortalised again and again in art and literature, from representations by male artists and writers, such as Rubens (1599), Yeats (1924) and Dali (1977) to feminist retellings in the 1990s by poets Lucille Clifton, Nina Kossman and Barbara Bentley. Many of us have heard of Leda and the Swan before, but might not have understood the myth's sinister origins. Leda was married to the king of Sparta and Clytemnestra's father, Tyndareus. Zeus was enthralled by her beauty so transformed himself into a swan pretending to escape from an eagle. In this form he raped and impregnated Leda, resulting in her laying an egg from which Helen was born. Some stories soften Zeus' crime to seduction, but Zeus had a bad habit of sexual violence. Besides, it's much more believable than being seduced by a swan.

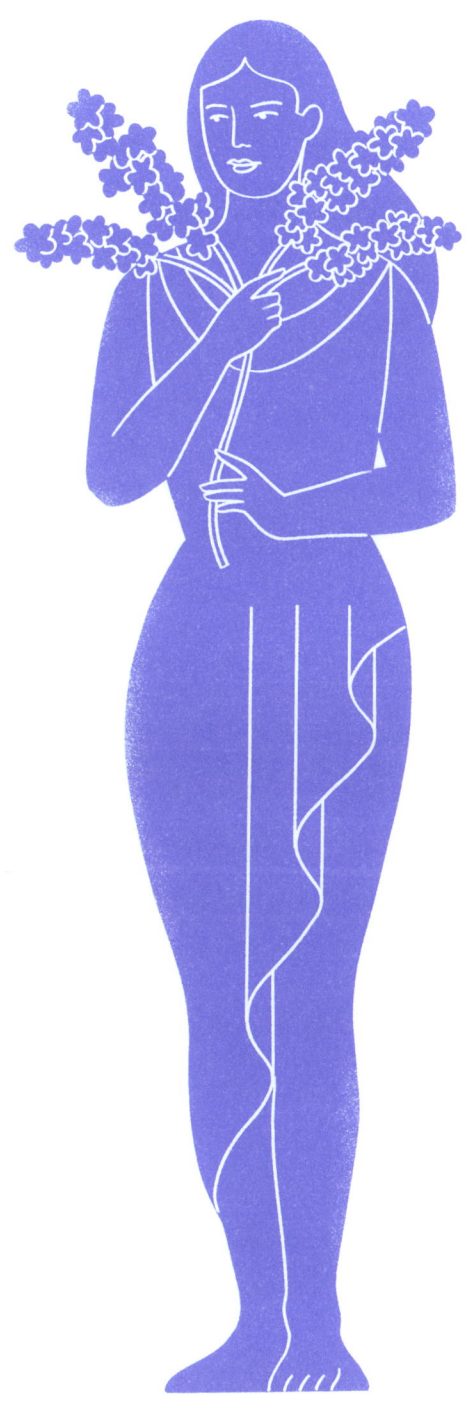

FEMME FATALE

FEMME FATALE

Leda was also impregnated by her husband the same night, resulting in four famous children: Helen, Clytemnestra, Castor and Pollux. Two were mortal and two were half divine, though which children were which varied. Helen is the only one consistently fathered by Zeus. In another variation, Zeus appeared to the goddess Nemesis as a swan and impregnated her, resulting in an egg which was given to Leda and hatched to become Helen. The myth has been retold by multiple, more contemporary, writers (including Sylvia Plath) who have used the myth as a lens to explore the status of women in their own context. The myth was used as inspiration in the popular science fiction television series *Orphan Black*, which focused on human cloning. In 2022, Hozier wrote the song 'Swan Upon Leda', in protest of the Supreme Court decision to overturn Roe v. Wade, taking away a woman's fundamental right to an abortion in the US. Imagery from the myth has even stolen the spotlight at Hollywood events – Marlene Dietrich famously wore a Leda and the Swan costume at a 1935 party (which inspired the infamous swan dress worn by Björk at the Oscars decades later).

Helen drew the unwanted attention of men from a very young age. Sometime before or around the age of ten (and possibly even as young as seven), she caught the attention of Theseus, who believed he was owed a divine wife because he was the son of Poseidon. Theseus kidnapped Helen as part of a bigger plot with Pirithous (who had set his sights on Persephone as a wife), before the two friends were thwarted by Hades in the underworld. On Earth, Helen's brothers Castor and Pollux invaded Athens and returned their sister to Sparta. As a Spartan girl, Helen had more of a physical education than girls from Athens. According to Ovid, she learnt to ride and hunt with her brothers and wrestled naked in the *palaestra*, which was a type of Greek wrestling school normally reserved for boys in other parts of Greece.

Many suitors (potentially up to forty-five men) came from all over the world to try and win her hand, but ultimately Helen's father chose Menelaus, a Spartan king, because he was the richest and most generous gift-giver. Helen's parents then abdicated, allowing her and Menelaus to take the throne. They had a daughter called Hermione who was just nine years old when her mother was either abducted or chose to leave for Troy. In some versions of the story, Paris legitimately won Helen's hand in marriage by proving to be superior, despite Helen's father seeking out Menelaus.

However, the most famous version of the story involves the so-called Judgement of Paris. Eris, the goddess of discord and strife, was offended she hadn't been invited to a wedding so threw a golden apple amongst the wedding party, labelled 'to the fairest'. Hera, Athena and Aphrodite all tried to claim it, so Zeus chose Paris to judge. Although it was difficult to decide, Aphrodite bribed Paris with an offer of the most beautiful mortal woman in the world, who was, of course, Helen. After that, events get a little hazy. Some say he abducted her, some say he raped her, and others claim Helen left willingly, perhaps swayed by lavish gifts. The idea that Helen might have even seduced Paris was also floated. But either way, it was her own fault that her beauty caused strife, right? Even Sappho, as a rare female voice from ancient Greece, seemed to blame Helen for deserting her husband and thoughtlessly leaving her daughter and parents. The blame attributed to Helen is evidence of the strict rules of duty and obedience real ancient Greek women were expected to abide by. Helen's was not an example to follow.

Menelaus requested help from his brother, Agamemnon, and the two of them waged war on Troy with many of the greatest Greek heroes, including Odysseus, Jason and Achilles. The Trojans blamed Helen for the war and grew to hate her, whilst Helen began to realise Paris' many faults and weaknesses, regretting what had transpired – although some authors, including Euripides, denied she ever made it to Troy, claiming that she hid out in Egypt for the duration of the war being waged to return her. Paris was killed in battle and she was given to his brother, Deiphobus. About the fall of Troy, we once again have different accounts. In one, she pretended to lead a chorus of Trojan woman in a bacchic rite, whilst in reality helping the Greeks to enter. In the *Odyssey*, she circled the horse imitating the voices of the Greek women the soldiers had left at home, which tortured the men inside. In another, she was panicked and alone as the city burns.

Ultimately, the Greeks won and Helen was returned to Menelaus, whether she wanted it or not. In the *Odyssey*, the couple have a somewhat harmonious reconciliation. Euripides has Helen returning to Greece to face a death sentence that never occurs, with Helen insisting that Aphrodite is to blame for her abduction. Other versions advocate for punishment, including hanging her from a tree, which later became a sanctuary. Recently, classical scholars with expertise in gender studies have highlighted that Helen can tell us very little about real women in the ancient world, but can tell us a lot about male attitudes towards them. Within the ancient Greek context, the perceived lasciviousness of a beautiful woman was often just a projection of male horniness. In modern works inspired by the myth, Helen's agency and sexuality have been central to the story as a conduit for feminist interpretations, including Lorde's song 'Helen of Troy' (2021) and Margaret Atwood's poem 'Helen of Troy Does Countertop Dancing' (1996), in which she is reimagined as an exotic dancer. Emily Wilson, the only woman to have published an English translation of the *Odyssey*, even suggested that society had been 'slut-shaming' Helen for centuries. There are still so many similarities between Helen's treatment in literature and misogyny in the media today that she is likely to endure as a symbol of women's position in society rather than for her objective beauty.

CLYTEMNESTRA:
THE DESPERATE HOUSEWIFE

Clytemnestra was the epitome of a bad wife – she had an affair with her husband's cousin and then murdered her husband. Her husband was Agamemnon, who was king of Mycenae and Odysseus' commander in the Trojan War. Unsurprisingly, Penelope and Clytemnestra are often highlighted as being the ultimate good and bad wife, respectively. Clytemnestra's half-sister (and wife of her husband's brother) Helen had been the reason for the war, either through being seduced or kidnapped by Paris, prince of Troy. Some scholars believed her name meant 'famed for her suitors', but in fact it is closer to 'celebrated conspirator'. However, considering her relationship history, her lack of loyalty to her husband is hardly surprising.

FEMME FATALE

Born a Spartan princess, Clytemnestra was the daughter of the king of Sparta and his queen, Leda (of the famed Leda and the Swan myth). According to Euripides' version of events, Clytemnestra had a first husband, who Agamemnon killed, along with Clytemnestra's baby boy. She went on to bear seven children to Agamemnon, including Iphigenia, Electra and Orestes. On his journey to Troy to retrieve his sister-in-law Helen, Agamemnon upset Artemis by killing a deer in her sacred grove, so she prevented him from reaching Troy unless he was willing to sacrifice his daughter, Iphigenia. Predictably, he was willing, but initially told his wife and daughter to send her to him so she could marry Achilles.

This family's tragic demise is documented particularly thoroughly in Aeschylus' dramatic trilogy, the *Oresteia*. He highlights Iphigenia's sacrifice as a key reason for Clytemnestra and her lover, Aegisthus, to murder Agamemnon. In this version Clytemnestra kills Agamemnon herself, whereas in older versions of the story, she persuades Aegisthus to carry out the deed. Agamemnon returned home from Troy after ten years with his mistress in tow, the Trojan princess Cassandra, whose prophecies nobody believed. Clytemnestra bided her time until Agamemnon decided to take a bath, cleverly trapping him in a fabric net so she could stab him to death. Afterwards, Clytemnestra remained queen for seven years, ruling alongside Aegisthus as her king until they were both murdered by Orestes, son of Clytemnestra and Agamemnon.

CALYPSO: LECHEROUS OR LONELY?

Calypso's only claim to fame, or rather the focus of the only surviving stories about her, was her concealment of Odysseus on her island for seven years – an additional seven years his wife Penelope had to wait faithfully for him to return. Like many of the other women in the *Odyssey*, Calypso is compared to Penelope and comes up short. She even enchanted Odysseus as she sang and wove on her own loom. So insatiable was her desire for him that she tried to detain him forever as her immortal husband – though one fragment of text suggests she kept him there on behalf of Poseidon, who hated Odysseus and tried his best to prevent him from returning home. No matter her reasoning, it was clear her primary purpose was as a plot device, considering her name literally means 'she who conceals'. Furthermore, she is often confused with the witch Circe, who also detained Odysseus, and there are differing accounts as to whether Odysseus' son Latinus was mothered by Circe or Calypso.

Although he initially enjoyed himself on Calypso's island, Odysseus began to lament for his wife, spending his days crying on the seashore for Penelope and his nights with Calypso, despite his protests. Athena begged Zeus to release him, for she did not have that power herself. Zeus sent the messenger god, Hermes, to order Calypso to let Odysseus go. She reluctantly gave him all the tools and materials he would need to construct a boat, but not before pointing out the hypocrisy of the gods, who could seemingly meddle with mortal women as they pleased but could not handle goddesses cavorting with mortal men. Because of this, she has fascinated post-classical philosophers and attracted the interest of women writers like Letitia Elizabeth Landon (known as the female Byron), whose 1836 poem 'Calypso Watching the Ocean' commented on the futility of Calypso forever pining for Odysseus' return. The poem is tinged with sadness for Calypso's lonely fate, a sentiment which Suzanne Vega's 1987 song 'Calypso' echoes. Despite the 'lonely time ahead', Vega's song instead moves towards acceptance for letting Odysseus go.

The question of whether Calypso was a villain is complex. Emily Wilson describes her as 'a passionate model of female power', along with Aphrodite and Circe. On the surface, she essentially held Odysseus against his will and forced him to have sex with her repeatedly, which we know is legally and morally wrong today. But in the ancient Greek context, these acts were considered wrong because it was a woman committing them against a man and not because they were considered wrong, fullstop. It was not unheard of for men to abuse their power against women, who were not even second-class citizens – they weren't citizens at all. Without a social model for how a powerful woman should behave, their behaviour in literature was modelled on powerful men, hence Calypso's sexual dominance over the hero of the epic poem.

Since ancient times, the 'femme fatale' has continued as a strong female archetype, but its meaning has shifted. Greek femme fatales mostly served as a warning to men and their medieval counterparts were meant to frighten women into behaving, whereas by the late nineteenth century, the femme fatale figure had become more titillating. During this period, she became associated with vampires, like in one of the original vampire novels *Carmilla* (1872), which has since become a lesbian classic due to the implied erotic desire between the vampire Carmilla and her female victim. The femme fatale had her true heyday during the film noir era of 1940s and 1950s Hollywood. She's also remained popular in more contemporary media, including Sarah Michelle Gellar's portrayal of Kathryn in *Cruel Intentions*; Rose McGowan as Courtney in *Jawbreaker* (both 1999); and Sherilyn Fenn's Audrey in *Twin Peaks* (1990). However, the ultimate femme fatale is still Aphrodite/Venus, who will forever be invoked in advertising, popular media and consumer products – just head to the women's shaving products in your local supermarket for proof!

Witch

Long before the stereotypical image of the broom-riding, cackling old crone, we had the sorceress of ancient literature who typically existed to control and punish men. The most notable ancient witches are Circe and Medea, yet these two are often remembered for their failures as women and mothers rather than their skills in the occult. Circe is known for interfering with Odysseus' journey home to his wife Penelope, and Medea for murdering her own children to exact revenge for her husband's new marriage. The 'problem' with these characters was not necessarily the fact that they were witches, but that they interrupted accepted gender roles. Traditionally, witches in art and literature represented 'incorrect' womanhood and served as a warning against women being allowed to defy gender expectations (or gravity), a tradition that is still alive in many children's stories and Disney movies. Many of our earliest sources for witches derive from ancient Greece, where they were usually seen as dangerously beautiful, another trope that reappears in fantasy today.

The Mother of Witches

HECATE

Hecate was the goddess of magic and witchcraft, as well as necromancy and spirits. In some stories Hecate was the mother of Scylla, and in others the mother of Circe and Medea, although Medea is more often depicted as a priestess or devotee of Hecate. Hecate was thought to be the daughter of the sun god Helios and Perse, one of the 3,000 Oceanides or water nymphs conceived by the Titans Tethys and Oceanus. Some believe that her cult spread from Anatolia and Egypt, perhaps related to the Egyptian word *heka*, meaning 'magic'.

In Greece and Rome, she was almost always depicted in her triple goddess form and was commonly found at a crossroads. In fact, her Roman epithet was Trivia, from Latin *triviae*, meaning 'three roads', which later came to mean 'commonplace' (hence our usage of trivial today). Ovid described her standing at the crossroads, with her faces looking in each direction. She was closely associated with Artemis/Diana, and some believed them to be two aspects of the same goddess before Artemis officially became an Olympian goddess (one of the twelve significant ancient Greek deities). Artemis represented purity, whilst Hecate was her dark side. The *Greek Magical Papyri*, a collection of spells, rituals and other magical research, indicate that Hecate held the keys to Tartarus, which is essentially the ancient Greek version of hell.

Artemis and Hecate both had a special connection with animals. Hecate was often accompanied by a dog, whose interpretation has evolved over time. In early depictions, the presence of the dog suggested a connection to childbirth due to its association with pregnancy and childbirth goddesses, including Artemis. Later, the dog was more suggestive of daemons or spirits. The dog is often female and appears to be friendly, much like a familiar. But the best version, told by Lycophron, relates back to the Trojan War. Hecuba, the queen of Troy, plunged herself into the ocean after the city's defeat and was turned into a dog with fiery eyes. She was left to rot in a place that can be translated as 'dog's tomb' before she was rescued by Hecate, who made her a familiar. The tradition of witches having animal familiars continues today, although women trapped in animal bodies thankfully seems to be less common.

Hecate was often portrayed holding twin torches, which played a key role in the Demeter–Persephone myth. In some tales, like the *Homeric Hymn to Demeter*, Hecate saw Hades abduct Persephone and used her torch to assist Demeter in searching for her daughter. The *Hymn* was composed sometime between the seventh and sixth centuries BCE and is one of our best sources for this myth. Due to her position at the crossroads between life and death, Hecate became a companion to Persephone and guided her between the underworld and the land of the living with her torches when it was time to reunite with her mother. Some even conflated Hecate with Persephone, or at least saw Persephone as one of Hecate's three iterations, and she was worshipped as an associate goddess of Persephone and Demeter at the centre of their cult worship at Eleusis.

The goddess Hecate is considered the original witch who was, and still is, depicted as triple-bodied, which is central to many neopagan practices. The three incarnations of the triple goddess represent the waxing, waning and full moon as well as stages in a woman's life: maiden, mother, crone. Unsurprisingly given her status, Hecate appears, or is called upon, frequently in popular culture, from leading the witches in Shakespeare's *Macbeth* to proclaiming herself queen of the underworld in *Charmed*.

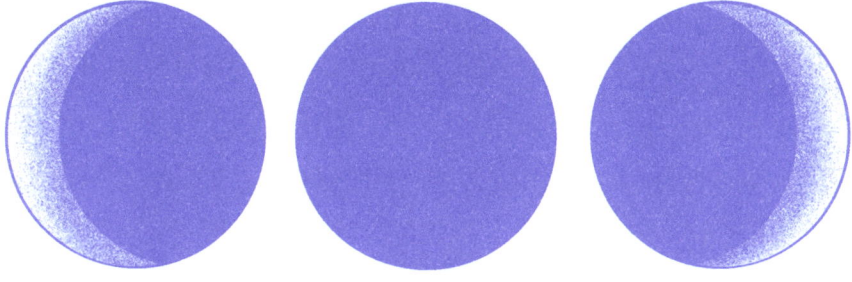

MEDEA AND MARRIAGE

Although Medea is primarily known today for murdering her children, her role as a sorceress was equally important in the ancient world as a renowned practitioner of *pharmakeia*, or medicinal magic. Medea's primary magical ability was tied to her cauldron, which had both rejuvenating and murderous uses. She was a granddaughter of Helios, niece of Circe and priestess of Hecate, from whom she drew most of her power. Despite her divine ancestry and magical prowess, she was mostly considered mortal in literature. Her good deeds included resolving a famine in Corinth, but she is rarely remembered for her charity.

Aside from committing infanticide, Medea still inspires empathy as the woman who risked it all for the man she loved, Jason, only to be betrayed. What is not often emphasised is that Aphrodite and Hera cast a spell on Medea to make her fall in love with Jason so that she could help him obtain the golden fleece and claim the throne. In fact, Jason only agreed to marry Medea because she offered her witchcraft expertise in exchange for marriage. And help him she did. Medea's father, Aeëtes, had been given the golden fleece for his kingdom years before. He agreed to give it to Jason if he could complete a series of impossible tasks that weren't so impossible with magic. During Jason's quest, Medea prepared a protection unguent, forewarned him of dangers through her talent of foresight, drugged a dragon and distracted her father by killing and dismembering her brother, to name a few of her little favours. Whilst her father was literally picking up the pieces, Medea and Jason ran off with the fleece. To atone for her fratricide, she paid her aunt Circe a visit, attended by nymph handmaidens. She made sacrifices and libations, calling on Zeus as the Cleanser, who lends an ear to murderers.

As depicted in Euripides' fifth-century BCE tragedy *Medea*, Jason abandoned her after ten years together for the king of Corinth's daughter. This drove Medea to complete despair. Her anguish might be understandable even without the love spell she was under, but its influence was too much to bear when she was thrown aside. She ended up sending Jason's new love, Glauce, a poisoned dress and crown, killing both her and her father (the king of Corinth), when he tried to save her. Following this, she killed two of her children and denied Jason their bodies. However, in some lesser-known versions of her story (like one told by the poet Eumelus), Medea never intended to kill her children but buried them alive in Hera's temple, erroneously believing it would turn them immortal.

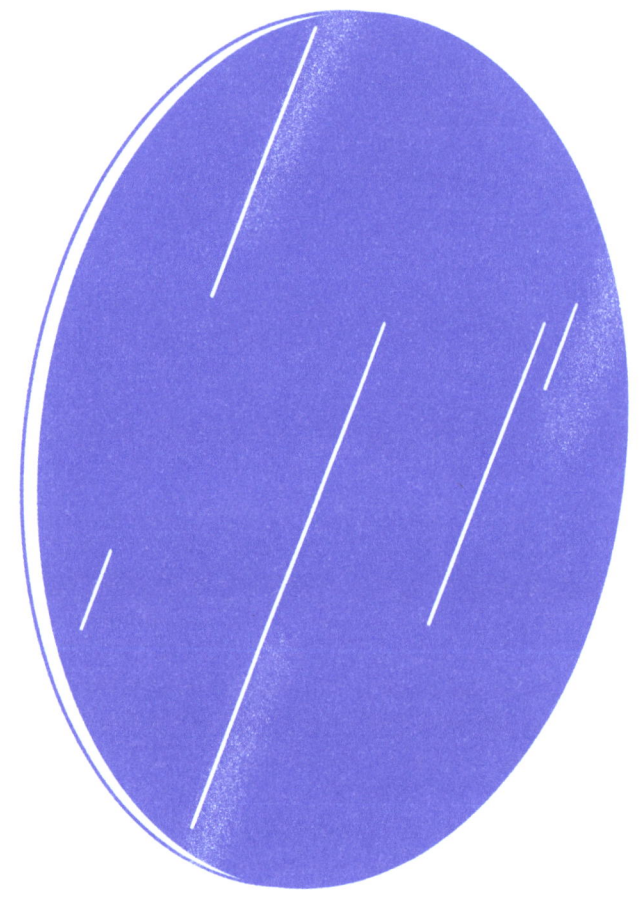

Medea not only served a purpose for Jason and the meddling gods, but she also served as a mirror for writers, performers and artists to reflect society. During the nineteenth century, Medea burst onto the popular British stage as a burlesque heroine who was able to emerge from tragedy (and her marriage) triumphantly. These Medeas often sprinkled in witty commentary about women's inferior position in both society and law, reflecting the parliamentary debates that were occurring around expanding women's very limited divorce rights and non-existent custody rights. Medea experienced a revival from the late 1990s onwards, as she was reinvented as a long-suffering and/or independent woman rather than a true villain. Her story has been told within the context of Dutch politics in a 2005 TV series, as well as modern-day Paris in a 2007 film *Médée Miracle*. In 1995 she appeared as a bisexual woman in the award-winning play *The Hungry Woman: A Mexican Medea* by Cherrie Moraga. Her story even inspired the 2015 British psychological thriller television series *Doctor Foster*, in which a doctor (the Medea character) gradually loses her mind as she investigates her husband's suspected infidelity, highlighting the mental anguish Medea suffered. As a doctor, she mirrors Medea's magic with her medical ability, but instead of killing her son, she just makes her ex-husband believe she has so he can feel her pain.

CIRCE'S COMEBACK

Circe was a sorceress and minor goddess, portrayed in classical literature as a warning for women going unchecked, and particularly of the dangers of excessive femininity to the patriarchy. Circe lived isolated from both gods and mortals on her own private island, Aiaia, attended by Naiads (sea nymphs) and Dryads (tree spirits). She is most famous for her relationship with Odysseus and his men (who she turned into pigs), but she has captured the imagination of many writers and artists over the years.

She was a very popular figure in Renaissance and Pre-Raphaelite art, and has recently had a renaissance of her own due to Madeline Miller's feminist retelling of her story. Circe has actually gained more momentum in popular culture than in her own context, becoming more popular today than she ever was in the ancient world. In the classical world, Circe was a villain, but so too were Amazons, (see page 91), with both witch and warrior intended to be negative examples of what could happen if women had complete freedom.

Most ancient stories about Circe revolve around her punishing men who rejected her. As well as turning Odysseus' men into pigs, she also famously turned the Italian king Picus into a woodpecker. Odysseus was only able to protect himself from transformation with his patron goddess Athena's help, sending Hermes with the mythical herb 'moly', which protected him against Circe's magic and poisons but didn't keep him from her bed. In fact, Odysseus uses her sexuality for his own benefit, gaining some favour with Circe through their sexual relationship. After he spends a year on her island, Circe eventually helps Odysseus and his men by bestowing them with nautical magic and instructions for returning home. At first she provides yet another delay to their journey, but ultimately helps them on their way, with Odysseus describing her as a 'great and cunning goddess'. Despite Odysseus' praise, authors like Ovid solidified the image of Circe as spiteful and jealous, inspiring nineteenth-century artists to paint her as either a femme fatale or vengeful, scorned woman.

But Circe didn't just take her revenge on men. She was also said to have poisoned the water nymph Scylla's bathing water, transforming her into a terrifying man-eating monster (see page 206). The reason for this? Circe fell in love with the sea god Glaucus, who in turn fell in love with Scylla. Whether or not Scylla even cared for Glaucus was irrelevant. In fact, in Ovid's version Scylla was so repulsed by Glaucus' love that she escaped up a mountain where he couldn't follow. He begged Circe for a love potion, and the rest is history. Or rather, mythology.

Over the years, women authors and artists have seen Circe as misunderstood. Possibly the earliest painting of Circe by a woman (or at least the most well-known) is Angelica Kauffmann's *Ulysses and Circe* (1786). It shows Circe as a more empathetic figure, reaching out to Odysseus, but still maintaining her position of power. Toni Morrison's 1977 novel *Song of Solomon* also features a Circe with dark beginnings, but who ultimately provides the main character with vital information. Madeline Miller's 2018 novel turns the whole Circe myth on its head and depicts her as a complex and powerful but neglected character with needs and desires that have never been met. Madeline Miller sensitively considered Circe's much-neglected perspective, exposing her emotional vulnerability and complicated relationship with men.

However, Circe's reception in the ancient world was more nuanced than extant literature might suggest. There were known to be small cults dedicated to Circe and she had a shrine at Mount Circeo in Italy. Worship often centred around pharmakeia, or the ancient art of sorcery and potion-making. It wasn't necessarily witchcraft that was considered problematic in the ancient world, but rather excessive or 'abnormal' womanliness.

QUEERING KURANGAITUKU

Far from Aeaea, we see some parallels with Circe in the story of Kurangaituku from Aotearoa (the original Māori name for New Zealand). There are multiple versions of the myth, which are particular to different *iwi* (or tribes) that still exist around the country. Kurangaituku was part-bird, part-woman and traditionally described as a witch, though some versions portray her more sympathetically as a protector or caretaker of birds. Like Circe, she was not the main character in her own story, but a well-known antagonist to the male hero, Hatupatu. Also like Circe, the dominant versions of the story describe Kurangaituku capturing Hatapatu whilst he was out hunting and imprisoning him in her cave along with her pet birds and reptiles. Some versions describe them as living together as a couple, whilst the version told by the Raukawa iwi shows Hatupatu illegally hunting in their (and Kurangaituku's) territory, where she finds him injured and cares for him. Either way, he eventually kills her beloved birds and escapes, leading her on a chase to the geothermal area of Rotorua, where she tragically died in the boiling mud and Hatupatu survived. Today, you can visit the mud pool where Kurangaituku supposedly met her end.

It is therefore no surprise that she has become a popular subject for reinterpretation by Māori women writers and artists, including contemporary artist Lisa Reihana and weaver Donna Campbell. Since the 1990s, she has graced the Rotorua travel centre in a collaborative artwork created by local women. She even appeared as the antagonist in a 2022 episode of *Wellington Paranormal* (a spin-off of the comedy-horror *What We Do in the Shadows*), in which she terrorises a modern descendant of Hatupatu and steals shiny objects from people's homes.

Kurangaituku has also become an icon to the queer and *takatāpui* community. *Takatāpui* is a word referring to Māori who identify as LGBTQ+ or gender diverse, a term which also derives from mythology. In 2019, Māori and lesbian activist Ngahuia Te Awekotuku reframed Kurangaituku as a nurturer, seeing her home as a kind of animal sanctuary that Hatupatu destroys. In this version, Kurangaituku does not die in the boiling mud, but uses the steam rising from it to hide, eventually enacting *utu* (the Māori concept of reciprocation and balance) on Hatupatu, taking away his voice for all the birdsong he eradicated.

But it is in Whiti Hereaka's 2021 novel *Kurangaituku* that she gets her most radical and sensitive transformation. Written to reflect long-established Māori oral traditions, the novel is non-linear in form. With her name shortened to Kura (a popular contemporary girl's name), she has become a *takatāpui* heroine, particularly to queer and trans women, ready to protect and even kill for them if necessary. The novel is also erotically charged, with Kura entering into a sexual relationship with Hine-nui-te-pō, goddess of the night. Although they don't get their happy ending, the depiction has been extremely important to the *takatāpui* community, which has a deep-rooted connection to the queer elements of Māori mythology and traditional culture.

Mythology and Gendered Persecution in Europe

As the classical era ended, the rise of Christianity bought a marked difference in the view of sorcery and witchcraft. Witchcraft changed from a practice seen as part of the natural order of things, to something dark, sinister and satanic.

After the Dark Ages came to a close, the so called 'witch craze' plagued Europe from the mid-fifteenth to mid-eighteenth centuries. The Dark Ages were named as such due to the artistic, intellectual and cultural decline following the collapse of the Roman Empire and classical period and the rise of Christianity and anti-pagan legislation. The Christian church systematically wiped out pagan art, literature, science and culture, destroying priceless masterpieces and knowledge and leaving ignorance in their place.

This history of persecuting witches is also intertwined with antisemitism. Jewish people were often accused of being demonic and spreading plagues and other evils, which was reflected in antisemitic art that went on to influence early depictions of witches, including exaggerated noses. There are even theories that the witch's iconic pointy hat derives from the *Judenhut* that Jewish men were required to wear in some parts of medieval Europe to identify themselves.

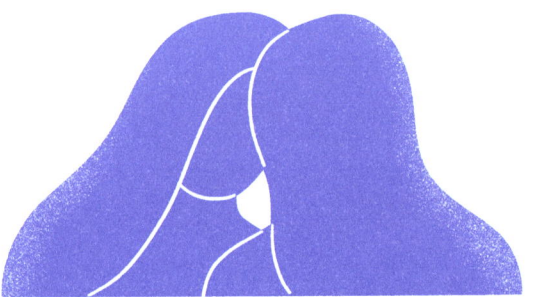

Those accused of witchcraft in this era were generally those that didn't fit gender expectations, including LGBTQIA+ people, disabled people and poor older women otherwise discarded by society. There was often a sexual element in the accusation of witchcraft, which could include sex with the devil or daemons as well as homosexual sex. Lesbianism was often considered actual proof of witchcraft, with several examples in Essex in the UK of women being hanged after accusations of being 'lovers and familiar friends'. We also have existing evidence of similar cases in Germany and France. In Spain, two nuns were burned alive during the sixteenth century for using 'material instruments' on one another, presumably medieval dildos.

Nuns actually come up surprisingly frequently in histories of witchcraft and sexuality. Some of the Salem witches hung in 1692 were also accused of inappropriate sexual behaviour, believed to be demonic in origin. There weren't many specific laws against lesbianism (unlike male homosexuality), but women could be punished for deviating from gender norms through accusations of witchcraft. Similarly, the sixteenth and seventeenth century witch trials were an opportunity to eradicate women that did not fit traditional roles.

The witchcraft that caused such panic was just a myth used by the church and those in power to manipulate people, but its impact was very real. Today, some women and queer people are drawn to witchcraft as a way of honouring those who have come before and draw inspiration from the occult as a personal practice or a symbolic tool for protest.

Madwoman

For millennia, men have dismissed women as overly emotional – even today, women's health concerns are often ignored and downplayed as being stress-related, hormonal or just in our minds. Madwomen are some of the most enduring female archetypes of the classical world. Descending from the same root, the word 'maniac' and the female group of 'raving ones' known as Maenads in ancient Greece have interconnected histories, highlighting how mania has long been considered a feminine flaw. From the ancient Maenads to *Jane Eyre's* madwoman in the attic to Florence Pugh's character Dani in the 2019 film *Midsommar*, the madwoman is an enduring trope. Even women's justifiable rage is presented as madness in many stories, which minimises genuine misogyny and inequality and blames it on women's supposedly inherent inability to cope emotionally.

Hysteria

As we've discovered in Chapter 1, sexist beliefs around women's mental and physical well-being led to centuries of misunderstanding. The Greeks and Romans used 'hysterical suffocation' to describe the feeling of heat and breathlessness caused by the wandering womb. Hysteria made a comeback as a medical diagnosis for women in the nineteenth century when strange ideas emerged about using orgasm as a cure, leading some doctors to use vibrators and devices on their female patients. Had so little changed in two thousand years? Fortunately, hysteria is no longer accepted as a medical diagnosis today. We are now aware of gynaecological conditions that could easily explain many of the symptoms mis-diagnosed as hysteria, like endometriosis, adenomyosis, PCOS and PMDD. However, as the concept of female hysteria was in itself pure misogyny, a diagnosis was often used as a tool for controlling women rather than a genuine effort to understand and help them.

Manic Maenads

The most famous maniacs of the ancient world are the Maenads, whose name comes from the same root word in ancient Greek *mainomai*, meaning 'to rave/to be mad'. They were followers of Dionysos who left their homes to live together in the wilderness and would ritually work themselves into a state of ecstatic frenzy, often with the help of drugs and alcohol. They were also very sexual beings and included orgies as part of their worship. Despite their collective identity, they were often singled out by name in art and literature. In Roman mythology they were known as *bacchae* or *bacchantes*, derived from Dionysos' Roman name, Bacchus.

Although most Maenads joined by choice, Dionysos did have the power to bend people to his will. In Euripides' play *The Bacchae*, Dionysos punishes his family for failing to recognise his divinity. Upon returning to his birthplace of Thebes, Dionysos was not received as a god by his cousin Pentheus, the king, nor by Pentheus' mother Agave. Not just the god of having a good time, Dionysos could be very vindictive when he didn't get his way. He cast a madness over all the women of Thebes, including his aunt Agave, causing them to roam the forests in endless revelry. In their madness, Agave and her Maenads hunted a lion, ripped it to shreds and carried its head back to the palace on a stick, only to realise the lion was actually Pentheus. Agave was either exiled or fled from Thebes, moved to Illyria to marry the king, and then eventually killed him.

Another group of Maenads tore Orpheus to shreds soon after his failure to rescue his wife Eurydice from the underworld, because he refused to entertain them and forsook his patron god Dionysos.

Despite such gory tales, Maenads are usually depicted in art as dancing maidens, a motif that remained popular until the early twentieth century. They are often shown in sheer clothing or a state of undress and sometimes in animal skin clothing, highlighting their wild nature. Their wildness even appears in *The Chronicles of Narnia*, where the Maenads 'began a dance, far wilder than the dance of the trees.' Their dancing poses in Greek and Roman art were extremely influential on female performers during the first half of the twentieth century. Maenads were reincarnated in modern dance through the likes of famous (or perhaps infamous) dancers Isadora Duncan and Maud Allan, whose often-frenzied movement imitated Maenads from Greek vase paintings. Duncan, who collected postcards of Maenads in Greek art, compared dancing to a Dionysiac ecstasy. Reviewers also noted the similarities, with one review calling Maud Allan a 'Maenad sister.' Allan gained notoriety for her personal life, especially when she tried to sue a British MP for libel when he publicly accused her of lesbianism (which turned out to be true) and collusion with the Germans (which was not true, as far as we know). The dancers' Maenad-like presence on the stage gave them a bad reputation in the media. Like ancient Maenads, they were considered guilty of untamed femininity, but their reverence for the ancient past resulted in modern dance techniques that eventually became standard.

Women of Lemnos, a land without men

Returning to the adventures of Jason and his Argonauts we arrive at the island of Lemnos, the origin of the phrase 'Lemnian deed', meaning to murder someone for revenge. When Jason and his men reached the island, they were very unusually greeted by women only. They soon found that all the 'male' jobs, like cow herding, blacksmithing and waging war, were occupied by women. Initially unsure whether to allow Jason's men into their manless city, the Lemnian women eventually invited them in on the advice of the queen's seeress, who suggested the women mate with their male visitors. The women explained to Jason's crew that they had been hit by a terrible plague, which had killed most of the men and caused the few remaining to flee.

However, the truth of the matter was that they had killed all the men for sleeping with (or perhaps raping) the Thracian women they had captured. Some stories say Aphrodite was directly responsible for this, adding another layer of revenge to the original Lemnian deed. In one version of the story, Aphrodite was furious that her husband Hephaestus had caught her cheating on him, so decided to punish his sacred island. In another version of the story, she punished the Lemnian women for neglecting to worship her by making them smell awful, causing their husbands to reject them. Whichever version you read, the one consistent element is that the women killed all the men. The king's daughter (and granddaughter of Dionysos and Ariadne), Hypsipyle, was made queen in his place. What the other women did not know was that Hypsipyle had secretly helped her father escape. When the other Lemnian women learned that Hypsipyle had betrayed them by saving her father, they either tried to kill her, sold her into slavery, or she fled and was captured by pirates, depending on who tells the story. In any case, the Lemnian women were used as an example of the world turned upside down, where women had taken a man's place and chaos reigned as a result.

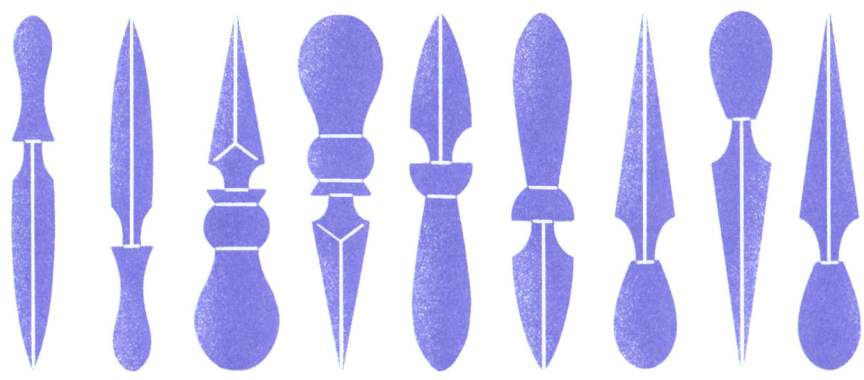

THE FURIOUS FURIES

The Furies (or Erinyes) were essentially goddesses of vengeance from the underworld. In art, they are depicted as ugly winged women who dressed either in the long black robes of mourning or in short tunics with boots similar to those worn by virgin huntresses like Artemis and Atalanta. Either way, like most of the women in this chapter, they did not represent socially acceptable femininity. These days, we mostly see the Furies portrayed as evil or frightening, but there was no need to truly fear them unless you had committed a truly terrible crime, like murder. Their punishments were particularly cruel but not undeserved. They were referred to euphemistically as the 'Kindly Ones' (or Eumenides) as it was considered ill-advised to mention them by name. Some stories present the Furies as numerous; others state there were three of them, each with their own attribute: Alecto's remit was anger; Megaera's department was jealousy; and Tisiphone dealt with vengeance for murder.

The Furies birth was quite unusual in that they emerged from the drops of blood spilt on the Earth when Cronos castrated his father Uranus and threw his genitals into the sea (from which Aphrodite emerged). Since they were born from patricide, they were particularly harsh in punishing those who killed a parent, afflicting the guilty with an unbearable madness. The Furies would not only inflict vengeance on the perpetrator but also punish any nation that might be hiding them, causing disease and starvation. In Aeschylus' tragedy *Eumenides*, the Furies viciously pursue Orestes for killing his mother, Clytemnestra (who had killed her husband, his father). After Orestes flees to Athens, the Furies threaten the Athenians and intend to poison the countryside. However, Athena proves to be too strong an opponent for the Furies and their vengeful plans are ultimately thwarted.

In alternative versions, the Furies were daughters of Nyx (goddess of the night) and possibly Hades, and there was also a religious sect that believed them to be the daughters of Persephone. Whether or not they were her children, the Furies were servants to Persephone and her husband Hades, torturing criminals sent to Tartarus, the Greek equivalent of hell. Vergil singles out Tisiphone as the guardian of the gates of Tartarus. She is usually portrayed as the most frightening of the three Furies, with snakes for hair and a dress dripping with blood. She used the breath of her hair snakes to incite madness, along with a poison concocted from Echidna's venom and Cerberus' drool. When a mortal man Cithaeron spurned her, she used one of her snakes to kill him. In Statius' *Thebaid*, she stirred up a war between Polynices and Eteocles and even drove one of the heroes, Tydeus, to cannibalism.

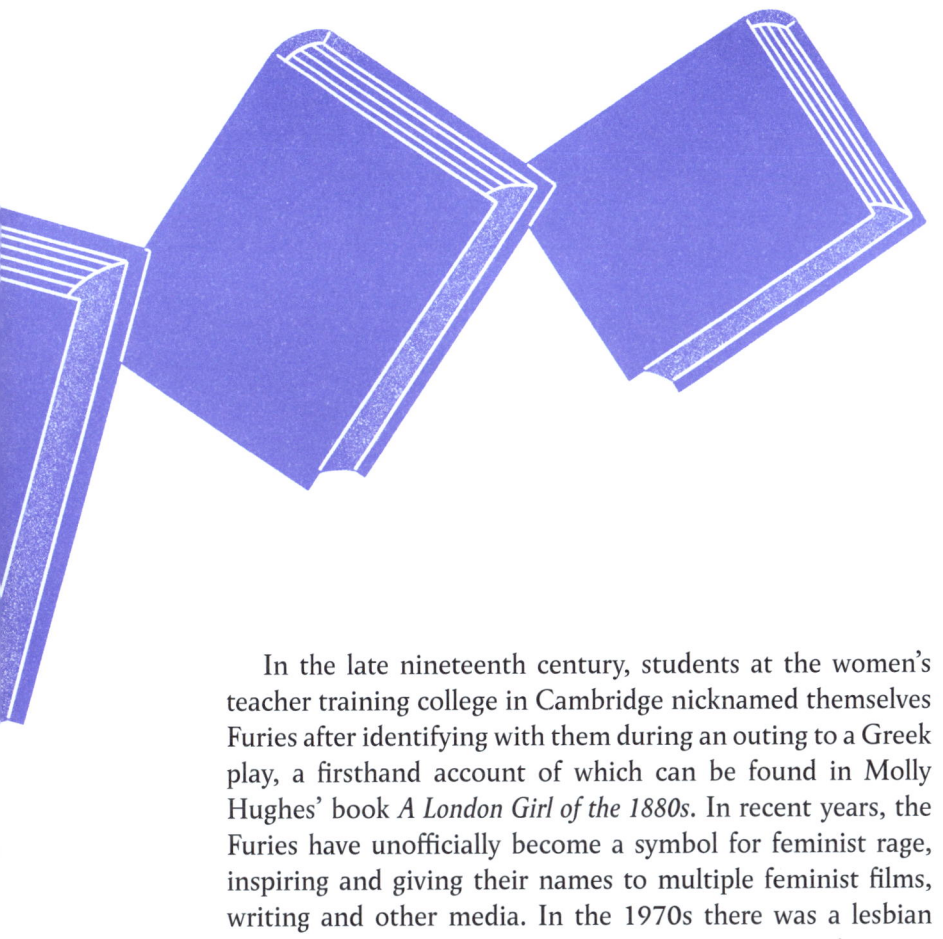

In the late nineteenth century, students at the women's teacher training college in Cambridge nicknamed themselves Furies after identifying with them during an outing to a Greek play, a firsthand account of which can be found in Molly Hughes' book *A London Girl of the 1880s*. In recent years, the Furies have unofficially become a symbol for feminist rage, inspiring and giving their names to multiple feminist films, writing and other media. In the 1970s there was a lesbian separatist group called the Furies Collective in Washington, D.C., whose publications were disseminated widely, inspiring the creation of other separatist groups globally. Netflix's *KAOS* also takes inspiration from 1970s lesbians in its depiction of the Furies, who are styled as Dykes on Bikes. DOB is a lesbian motorcycle club that originated at San Francisco Pride in 1976 and now has chapters around the world, including Sydney, where they play a prominent role in Mardi Gras. American poet Evie Shockley, whose work engages with the Black Lives Matter movement, called her poem about the tragic death of Breonna Taylor at the hands of the police: 'breonna taylor's final rest (or, the furies are still activists). The poem invokes Tisiphone by name to hunt down justice for Breonna.

THE CASSANDRA COMPLEX

In yet another tragic tale of a mortal woman wronged by a god, Cassandra, a Trojan princess and priestess, was eventually driven mad by Apollo, who she had the audacity to reject. He had taken a fancy to her and offered her prophetic powers, which she gladly accepted. There are contradictory versions of events – in one, Cassandra promised herself to Apollo in exchange for her new talent but reneged; in another, Apollo did not declare his intention to bed her and decided to punish her when she rejected him. Instead of withdrawing Cassandra's power to predict impending doom, Apollo cursed her to never be believed. Cassandra made multiple important predictions regarding the Trojan War that were totally ignored, much to the Trojans' detriment. You see, she could have prevented the war in the first place if her brother Paris had heeded her warning about Helen (not that it was difficult to predict that stealing a king's wife from the city-state with the strongest military in Greece would cause some issues). She attacked Helen after she arrived in Troy, even trying to rip her hair out, which didn't exactly help her reputation as someone who was a bit unstable. She warned her fellow Trojans about the wooden horse, and still, nobody listened. After Troy fell, she was taken as a concubine by Agamemnon (Clytemnestra's husband) and eventually murdered by Clytemnestra with full foresight of her fate. Unsurprisingly, Cassandra's curse unraveled her sanity, pushing her more and more frequently into a manic state. She is often referred to as manic or compared to a Maenad by other characters in her story – Ovid tells us that Agamemnon noticed both her beauty and wild Maenad-like hair.

Today, a 'Cassandra complex' (or syndrome) describes situations where disaster could have been averted if people were willing to listen. It is used in psychology and also applied to people's inability to believe science and willful ignorance regarding environmental issues. The Cassandra complex has also fascinated writers and filmmakers: 2021's *Don't Look Up*, a satirical take on an impending apocalypse, serves as an allegory for climate change. Autistic author Holly Smale (known for the YA series *Geek Girl*) published her first adult novel *The Cassandra Complex*, which uses the Cassandra myth as an insight into the struggle to be heard as an autistic person. She also exists as a television trope – a woman with foresight who is often perceived to be crazy or, at the very least, belittled. In *The Magicians*, the original Cassandra has become immortal and appears as a scribe whose prophetic ability has been industrialised to write all the books of people's lives before they've lived them. She is unable to relate to 'normal' people, causing frustration on both sides.

From a feminist perspective, Cassandra's story has become an allegory for women's precarious position in a patriarchal society. She had the bravery to reject not just a mortal man but a god, and was punished for it. Her very real concerns were ignored. In 1852, before she became famous as the founder of modern nursing, thirty-two-year-old Florence Nightingale wrote a feminist essay that served as a thinly veiled autobiography about her lot in life. She called the essay *Cassandra*, and in it, she fiercely critiques a woman's powerless position in the Victorian family. Cassandra also had a feminist moment during the #MeToo movement due to the similarities between her story and the countless incidences of abuse that were shared by survivors online.

The Original Wicked Stepmother

HERA

Despite being the goddess of marriage, women and childbirth, Hera is more renowned for her cruel and vengeful behaviour than her maternal instinct. For that reason, she is often depicted as a madwoman and the cause of many curses and punishments inflicted on lesser gods and mortals. Her reputation as a 'mean girl' has lasted the test of time and we often see her as an unnecessarily ruthless adversary. Her acts of revenge were usually carried out on her husband Zeus' lovers and illegitimate children. She could be seen as the original wicked stepmother made popular in fairy stories and Disney films, though ironically, she does not take on this role in Disney's *Hercules*. Her brand of vengeance included trying to kill baby Hercules; kidnapping the goddess of childbirth to try and stop Leto giving birth to Artemis and Apollo; punishing the Trojans because Paris chose Aphrodite as the most beautiful goddess; and bereaving Lamia of her children, causing her to become a child-eating monster. She even threw her own son, Hephaestus, from Olympus, either because of, or causing, his disability.

However, the humiliation and hurt she suffered at the hands of her husband is often ignored or downplayed to make her reactions seem unfounded and extreme. Whilst her acts of retribution are unusually cruel, she also suffered violent treatment from her husband (who was also her brother) and she might not have even consented to marry him in the first place, according to some authors, including the famous Greek historian Plutarch. She hasn't had as many feminist reappraisals as similar mythological women, but we must understand that she reflects the limited options women had in classical society. Despite being queen of the gods and the second most powerful Olympian after Zeus, she was still denied rights as a woman and was beholden to her husband, unable to either prevent his infidelity and brutish behaviour or to leave him.

Madwomen in mythology have often reflected complex emotions that real women in history did not have the framework to express. These emotions were often caused by the actions of men around them or the callousness of the gods. Whilst we might judge the way these characters tried to process their pain, they still have a lot to tell us about the plight of women in both the ancient world and today, when women are so often pitted against each other professionally, romantically and socially. These 'madwomen' have so much to say about how women's emotions have been used as weapons against them, especially when they are purposely pushed towards their absolute limit. If only society would listen to them.

Monster

The majority of monsters in the ancient world were female, reflecting a societal fear of women with any sort of power, but especially power over men. From Echidna, the so-called mother of all monsters, to the Sirens, the enduring symbol of male temptation, these monsters were designed to push the narrative that women who went unchecked were dangerous. Many of them did not start out as monsters but as beautiful women who were punished by the men who were attracted to them. Although some versions of the myth depict Medusa as one of three monstrous sisters known as 'Gorgons', in the more enduring version by the Roman poet Ovid, Medusa was turned into a monster by Minerva to punish her for being raped by Neptune in her temple. Scylla, the man-eating monster featured in Homer's *Odyssey* and Vergil's *Aeneid*, was once a beautiful sea nymph who was turned into a monster out of jealousy – in some stories by another sea nymph and in others by Circe herself. Monsters are some of the most fascinating female characters from ancient mythology because they are often the most misunderstood and victimised.

Villains or Victims?

MEDUSA

The monsters of classical mythology were mostly women who were in the wrong place at the wrong time. Arguably the most enduring monster is the snake-haired Medusa, who could turn men to stone with her gaze. Her iconic image is the subject of countless paintings; the symbol of luxury fashion house Versace; has featured in multiple adaptations (including Rick Riordan's *Percy Jackson* series and Natalie Haynes' novel *Stone Blind*); and has, more recently, become a feminist icon. She has unofficially been named the face of feminist rage; you can even buy Medusa-adorned T-shirts with the slogan 'Petrify the Patriarchy'. With her deadly stare, she is the ultimate subversion of the male gaze and has been used to express fury, empowerment and female sexuality, both due to her desirability before her monstrous transformation and in reclaiming ownership of her body as a survivor of sexual assault. Rihanna even famously appeared as Medusa in the twenty-fifth anniversary edition of the men's magazine *GQ*. Many of you may remember the sculpture of victorious Medusa by Luciano Garbati that went viral in 2018 and was then recreated outside a Manhatten courthouse, showing a nude Medusa carrying the decapitated head of Perseus – the man who beheaded Medusa in original versions of the myth. She's even been treated to sapphic reimaginings in art and literature in recent years, and lesbian Medusa has become a popular trope in sapphic communities online, especially when pairing Medusa with a blind woman.

Medusa's longevity in popular culture is originally related to Ovid's interpretation of the myth in his influential narrative poem *Metamorphoses*. In the poem, Medusa wasn't born a monster, she was a beautiful young woman who caught the attention of Poseidon. Poseidon raped her inside one of Athena's temples, and instead of punishing the perpetrator of the crime, Athena turned Medusa into the monstrous form we are familiar with. As one of the most powerful gods and Zeus' brother, Athena was unable to punish Poseidon in the same way, and punishing the woman for a man's violence is something of a tradition in Greek mythology anyway. Some believe that Athena was surreptitiously protecting Medusa from Poseidon and men in general. This story inspired later artists to highlight both the beautiful and beastly aspects of Medusa's appearance, while early Greek depictions show her as a tongue-baring monster known as a Gorgoneion. Like the evil eye talisman today, the Gorgoneion motif was believed to ward off evil. If you look closely at a statue of Athena, you should be able to see the face of Medusa on Athena's aegis (a shield-like garment), which she placed there after Perseus gave her Medusa's decapitated head. Its protective quality was so strong that not even Zeus' thunderbolt could pierce it. Medusa was pregnant with Poseidon's child at the time of her murder, and the winged horse Pegasus and his sword-wielding giant of a brother, Chrysaor, emerged from her body upon her death.

In the late nineteenth century, Medusa was transformed into a 'femme fatale' by reactionary voices in response to the nascent women's empowerment movement, along with the Sirens and Sphinxes. She also garnered sympathy from feminists, and women artists began to portray her more tenderly in their work, in contrast to her monstrous classical interpretations. Alice Pike Barney used her daughter as the model for Medusa in her haunting 1892 painting of the same name. She wanted to tell Medusa's story from a woman's perspective and invoke sympathy for her tragic ending.

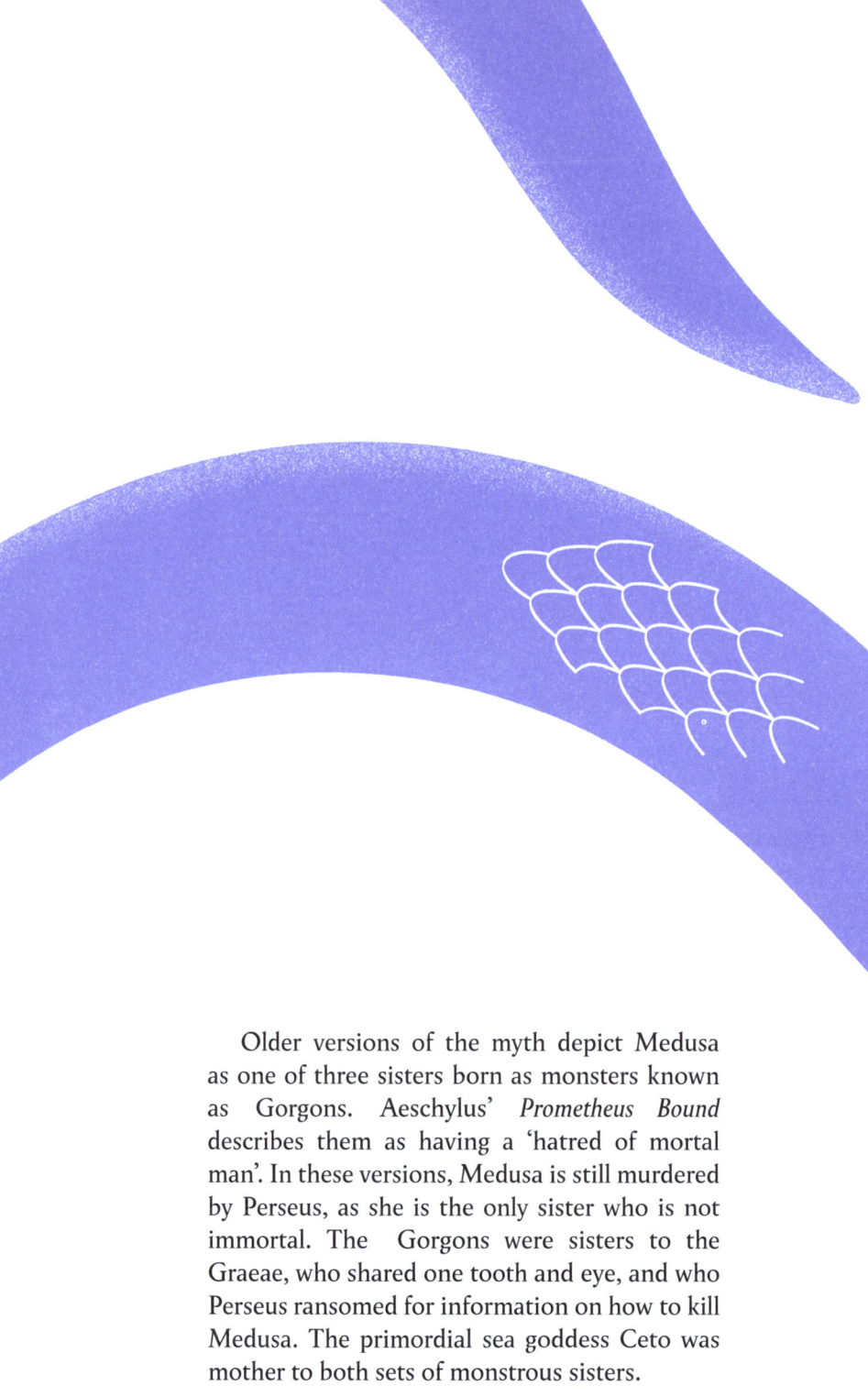

Older versions of the myth depict Medusa as one of three sisters born as monsters known as Gorgons. Aeschylus' *Prometheus Bound* describes them as having a 'hatred of mortal man'. In these versions, Medusa is still murdered by Perseus, as she is the only sister who is not immortal. The Gorgons were sisters to the Graeae, who shared one tooth and eye, and who Perseus ransomed for information on how to kill Medusa. The primordial sea goddess Ceto was mother to both sets of monstrous sisters.

Water, Women and Woe

CETO

Ceto was one of the first generation of deities, who symbolised some of the larger elements of life and the universe. Her name can be translated literally as 'sea monster' and she was the daughter of Gaia, *the* Mother Earth. She represented all sea monsters, including large sea creatures like whales and sharks. But most significantly, she represented the dangers of the sea – the first of many mythological oceanic women who caused the downfall or death of many a man foolish enough to stray into her territory. It certainly speaks to the view of women held by men in ancient Greece and Rome that any perils at sea were largely blamed on women, simply because they understood the mysteries of the ocean about as much as they understood women and their biology. Like most of the primordial deities, Ceto was not known to have been actively worshipped, though unusually for a goddess of her kind, some scholars believe that there was a cult dedicated to her in the port of Joppa (now Jaffa).

In addition to Medusa and her sisters, Ceto was also mother and grandmother to a whole host of monsters, including the grey-haired Graeae, Ladon the dragon and Echidna, who was mother to most of the famous monsters in classical mythology, including Scylla.

BETWEEN *Scylla*

Similar to Medusa, the most enduring versions of Scylla the sea monster's story depict her as a beautiful naiad (or freshwater nymph) who was turned monstrous due to the jealousy of another. In early commentaries on Vergil's *Aeneid*, she was chosen by Poseidon and transformed by the sea nymph Amphitrite, whereas in other versions (such as by the Latin author Hyginus), she was beloved by Glaucus who was in turn beloved by the witch Circe. In both versions, the jealous woman poured poison into the water where Scylla bathed, turning her into a monster of varying descriptions – she is most commonly depicted as having multiple heads or dogs sprouting from her legs. Scylla guarded one side of a narrow strait, thought to be the real-life Strait of Messina in Italy. She lay in wait opposite Charybdis, another sea monster who started life as a woman and was punished by Zeus, who expelled her to the bottom

AND *Charybdis*

of the sea. There are variations on why she was punished, but the most common version is that she aided her father, Poseidon, in his feud with Zeus and besieged the land with her forceful waters. In another version, she was known to be rapacious and stole the cattle of Herakles (Zeus' son). Again, her appearance varies, but most viewed her as a giant whirlpool, responsible for the tides.

Charybdis created whirlpools by swallowing ocean water, making it an extremely perilous, nearly impossible, ordeal for men to cross in their ships. Homer described the horror of encountering her vividly, narrating that 'She seethed and swirled through all her depths like a cauldron set on a great fire.' However, if they sailed too far away from Charybdis, Scylla would eat the men alive.

MONSTER

This story, made famous by Homer, is thought to be the origin of the phrases 'between a rock and a hard place' and the 'lesser of two evils', which was historically expressed through the proverb 'between Scylla and Charybdis'. Our first recorded acknowledgement of the phrase as a proverb can be found in Erasmus' *Adagia* (1515) and it has been used frequently in literature over the centuries. More recently it has appeared in song lyrics, including the Police's 1983 single 'Wrapped Around Your Finger', and Trivium's 2008 heavy metal song 'Torn Between Scylla and Charybdis'.

All stories of Scylla and Charybdis centre around men, because all of the mythological stories about seafaring are about men, reflecting the strict gender roles in ancient Greek society. These monstrous women, on the other hand, are often used as plot devices to highlight the skill and civility of men. One of the Greek heroes who had to make this treacherous choice between Scylla and Charybdis was Odysseus (of Homer's *Odyssey*), who faced many women on the margins of society on his journey home from Troy to his wife Penelope (who, as we have seen, was presented as the ideal Greek wife). Prior to leaving Circe's island (see page 160), Circe advises Odysseus to sail closer to Scylla than Charybdis, as it would be better to lose men than the entire boat. Odysseus follows this advice and loses six men to Scylla's six heads.

There aren't many mythological tales of female cooperation, but it could be said that Scylla and Charybdis worked together to achieve a common goal – the destruction of men. It would also seem that men could only pass successfully with the help of a woman – in Odysseus' case Circe, and for Jason and the Argonauts, the sea nymph Thetis. In Vergil's *Aeneid*, Juno (the Roman queen of the gods) positioned herself against the protagonist Aeneas and fought with her husband Jupiter over him. She tried to use Scylla and Charybdis against him and, lamenting their failure, then tried to incite a war to kill him off.

SIRENS VS MERMAIDS

Women were blamed for many of the sea's dangerous mysteries. Perhaps an even more enduring myth than Scylla and Charybdis is that of the Sirens, who also appear during Odysseus' arduous journey home. They were thought to be the daughters of the river god Achelous and one of the muses. People often think of Sirens as mermaid-like in appearance, but they were first depicted in art and literature as women–bird hybrids with varying degrees of human and birdlike features – usually the body of a bird with the head of a human. Greek artists would occasionally depict Sirens with fishtails and human top halves, but it was only during the Middle Ages that the mermaid appearance stuck. Either way, the Sirens are certainly crucial to the origin of later mermaid folklore, along with other Greek and Roman, Teutonic (ancient Northern Europe), Mesopotamian (ancient Iraq), and ancient Syrian mythologies.

Numbering between two and eight, Sirens would lure sailors to their deaths with their alluring singing. More recent depictions present the Sirens as seductresses, using their sexuality to lure men to their deaths, away from their wives, or even simply just to rob them as in the film *O Brother, Where Art Thou?*, based on *the Odyssey*. Odysseus only survives his experience with the Sirens because of Circe's advice. He ordered his men to plug their ears with beeswax and, wanting to hear the song that was the downfall of many a man, requested that his men tie him to the mast of the ship and keep him there until the Sirens were out of earshot. Jason and his Argonauts had the celebrated musician Orpheus aboard their vessel, so they used Orpheus' beautiful music to drown out the sound of the sirens.

Ovid's *Metamorphoses* offers a compelling interpretation of the Sirens as women supporting women. As the constant companions of Persephone, they were able to enjoy female friendship in peace, unmediated by meddling men. Until Hades entered the picture, that is. In fact, according to Ovid, Persephone's plight motivated the Sirens to become the fearsome creatures they are known as. After witnessing her abduction by Hades, they searched the land with Demeter, desiring to grow wings so they could cross the seas. Their loyalty so moved the gods that they bestowed the Sirens with golden plumage over their bodies but preserved their human heads to maintain their enchanting voices.

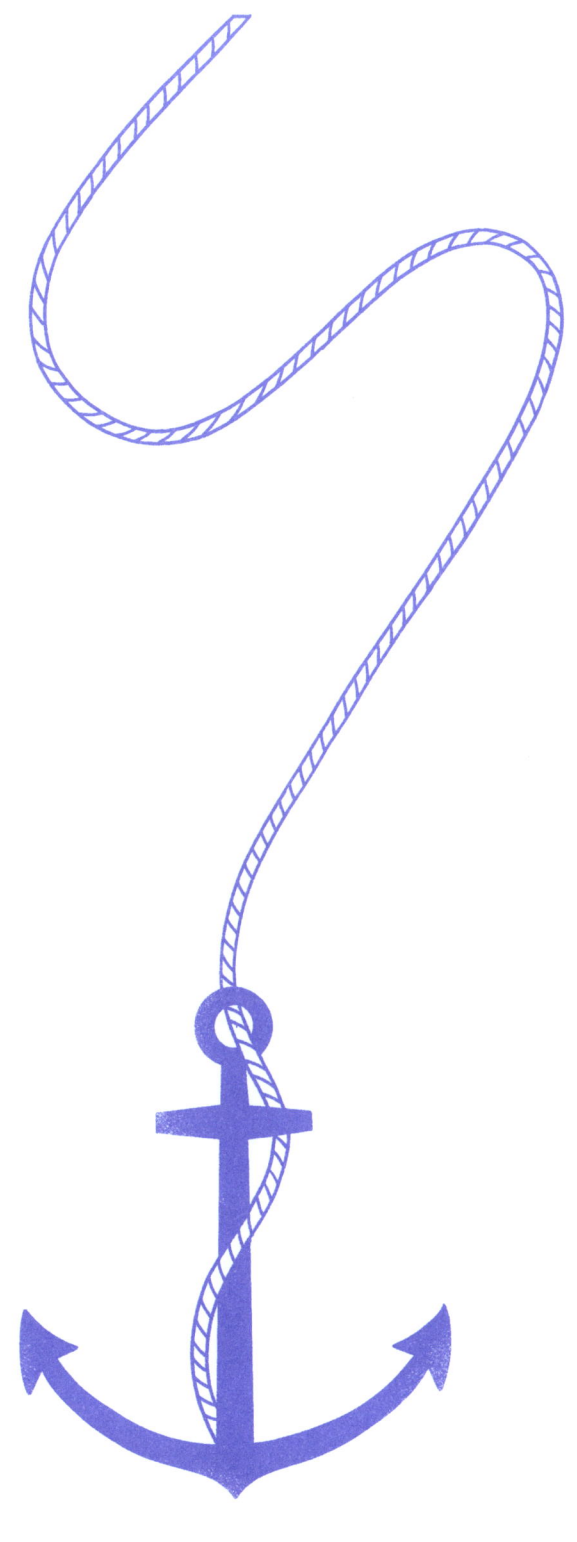

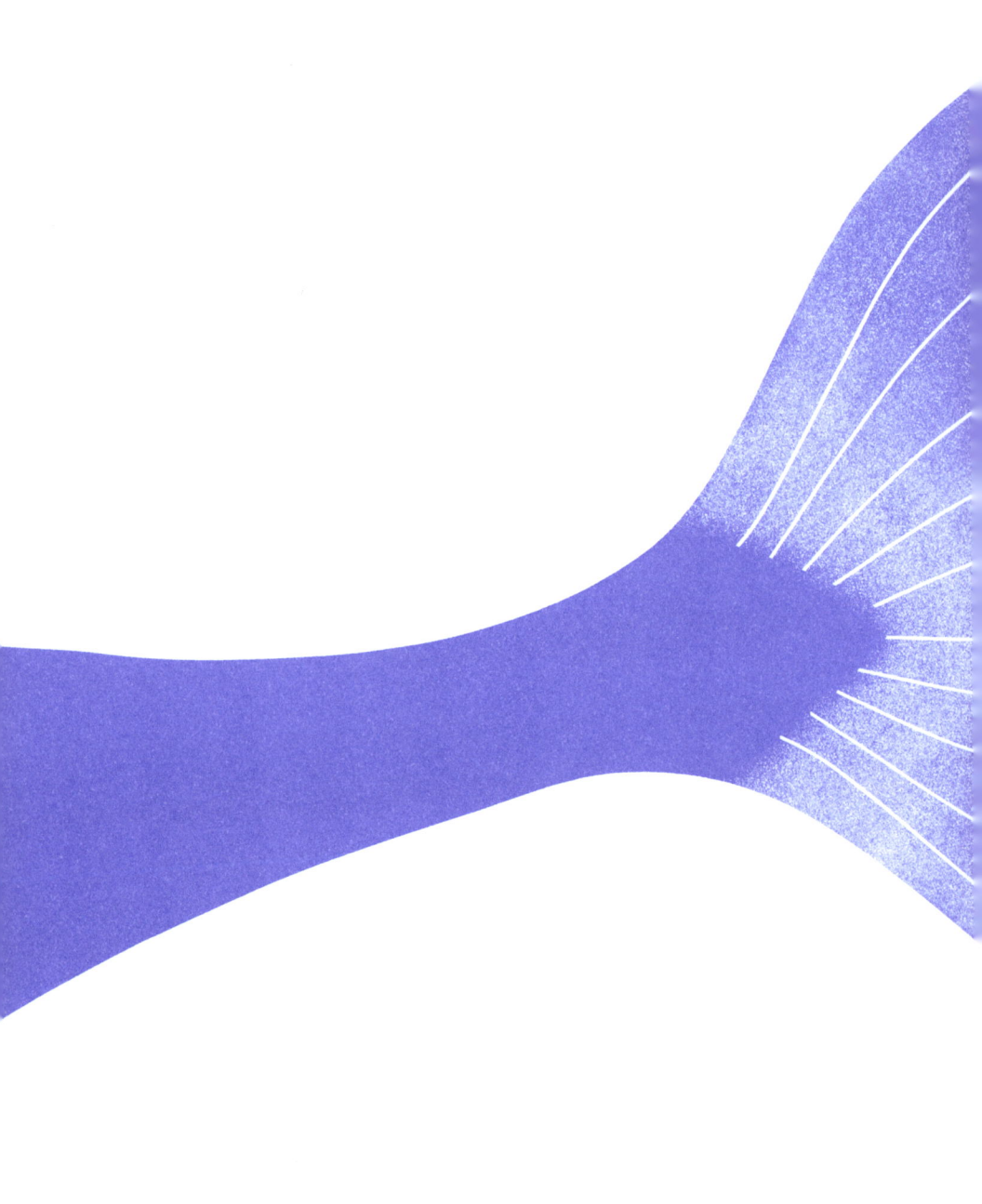

Medieval mermaids took on many of the negative feminine qualities of Sirens, and although the stories vary across Europe, they were commonly seen as unlucky or dangerous. In Eastern Europe, mermaids were thought to be women who had died tragically, usually by murder or suicide, before marriage. They danced together under the moon, luring men to their deaths in the water. In Western Europe, intense misogyny, combined with the transition from pagan to Christian practices, meant that mermaids were not only considered evil, but they also began to appear frequently in church iconography to symbolise the sins of lust and pride. Due to low literacy levels, many church-goers would be more familiar with the image of the mermaid than the text of the bible itself. The earliest known depiction of a mermaid in England comes from the Norman Chapel at Durham Castle (ca. 1087), but today it is hard to view this adorable stubby mermaid in the threatening way it was initially intended. Monstrous mermaid 'specimens' became popular in European collections and museums during the 1800s, corresponding with the rise of inherently racist and ableist 'freak shows'. These specimens were actually hybrid taxidermy pieces, usually combining sea creatures with monkeys.

I want

to

be

where

the

people

are

You may wonder how we ended up with the human-loving Ariel as our most well-known representation of a mermaid after centuries of tales warning humans away from their allure. Disney's *The Little Mermaid* was loosely based on Danish author Hans Christian Andersen's fairytale 'The Little Mermaid' (1837), which was in turn based on layer upon layer of European mermaid mythology and folklore, as well as the German fairytale *Undine* (1811). There are instances of friendly mermaids in very specific places, such as the ben-varrey from the Isle of Man, but the reception of mermaids overall cannot be separated from the way women were viewed in their geographical and chronological context. Hint: not very positively.

Hans Christian Andersen's story became so popular that a Little Mermaid statue was unveiled in Copenhagen in 1913 and the idea of the benevolent, human-loving mermaid has remained in our imaginations ever since. By the twenty-first century, mermaids had become a popular symbol for transgender people, with the UK's largest charity for trans and gender nonconforming youth taking the name Mermaids. Many trans and queer people identify with mermaids' themes of transition and transformation. Modern scholars have also interpreted Hans Christian Andersen's original story through a lens of gender fluidity and queerness, with some viewing mermaid stories as coming-out stories. Some even suggest that Hans Christian Andersen might have been a closeted trans person or at least queer in some way, and there is even evidence that could point to the story being an allegory of his sexuality or gender identity. Letters suggest that the story was dedicated to a particular male companion, with Hans Christian Andersen writing to him, 'The femininity of my nature and our friendship must remain a mystery.'

Andersen drew from the selkies of Norse and Celtic mythology, who actually have more similarities to modern-day mermaids than Greek Sirens, despite being lesser known. Instead of being half and half, selkies could shapeshift between human and seal form, often by removing their sealskin. They are not categorically good or evil, and could help or hinder humans depending on circumstances. Unlike Greek Sirens and early mermaids, there are more stories of selkies being harmed by men than the other way around. In these tales, men would steal and hide a selkie's shed sealskin so that she was trapped with him on land and forced to become their wife. In some cases, selkies eventually found their sealskins and returned to the ocean for their happily ever after.

Historically, many indigenous cultures practised more fluid beliefs about gender, sexuality and the status of women than ancient Greeks or Romans. It comes as no surprise that these cultures include powerful but mostly benevolent female water spirits who provide essential elements and protection to humankind, rather than punishment. Understandably, they occasionally seek retribution when wronged, or if the resource they protect is threatened. These mythological beings include the yawkyawk freshwater spirits of the Kunwinjku people in Australia, who have life-giving powers; the Ala-Muki river dragon-woman from Hawai'i, who provided nourishment; the Inuit goddess Sedna, who became the mother of the sea and sea creatures; and the Brazilian/African goddess Iemanjá from the Vodou tradition, who was a mother of the water and gods as well as the patron saint of sailors.

Like Mother Like Daughter

ECHIDNA

Similar in appearance to a mermaid, the half-snake, half-woman Echidna was considered the mother of monsters. Her offspring included many of the most fearsome beasts in Greek mythology. She birthed Scylla (according to Vergil's *Aeneid*), multiple dragons, the Hydra, Cerberus (the three-headed dog guarding the gates of the underworld), the Chimera and the Sphinx, to name a few. Hesiod described her as having a beautiful, nymph-like woman's face, whereas other sources depict her as hideous or even many-headed, with a dangerous venom. She lived alone in an underground cave, and most of the surviving stories about Echidna focus solely on the monstrous children she produced, maintaining that unshakeable theme in Greek mythology that women not only represent but cause all that is wrong in the world. Her role as a mother is also emphasised in *Percy Jackson*, where she is labelled 'the Mother of Monsters' in both the book and TV series. She appears as an unassuming middle-aged woman enticing her monstrous children to attack, especially the Chimera, who always accompanies her disguised as a chihuahua with a rhinestone collar. She hasn't gained the same status in popular culture as some of her daughters, but she has given her name to a small Australian and New Guinean animal with coarse hair and spines. It is one of the only egg-laying mammals. Hence, people originally believed it had both mammal and reptile qualities, like the monster Echidna.

CHIMERA

The Chimera had three heads – those of a lion, a goat and a snake – and breathed invincible fire. She terrorised Lycia (in Turkey) and some later classical writers theorised that she symbolised the active geothermal area there, now called Mount Chimaera, which produced fires from gases escaping the rocks. Based on historical reports, the area also had lions, goats and snakes, which could explain the bizarre appearance of the Chimera. Similar to the sea monsters, unknown and otherwise inexplicable natural dangers were attributed to a female monster. She was, of course, heroically killed by a man, Bellophoron, who had also captured Medusa's son Pegasus.

The word 'chimera' (with a lower case 'c') entered the English language to describe a fantasy, delusion or illusion of the mind, particularly relating to an unrealised dream. The Chimera appears frequently in manga, anime and video games in its traditional monstrous form (or a variation of it), such as *Yu-Gi-Oh!*, and is named symbolically in various movies, like *Mission Impossible 2*, as well as sci-fi and crime television shows including *The X-Files, Star Trek* and *NCIS*. In *Mission Impossible 2,* Chimera is a virus, and Bellophoron is the cure. *Star Trek: Deep Space Nine* has an episode named 'Chimera' because of a changeling that features in the episode, referring to the Chimera being multiple species at once. A Chimera even appears in the children's animation *My Little Pony* as an antagonist who is a tiger/snake/goat hybrid. Perpetually mysterious, the Chimera has endless allegorical possibilities that allow her to remain timeless, even in scientific fields. In genetics, chimerism refers to a condition that causes a human or animal to have at least two sets of differing DNA. The American Psychological Association defines 'chimera' as 'an illusion of the imagination, sometimes something desired but impossible to realize,' a meaning which has filtered into popular culture.

SPHINX

When conjuring up the image of a sphinx, most people automatically think of the Great Sphinx of Giza. However, the Egyptian sphinx is not a true sphinx; but rather the name attributed to it during the Greek and Roman classical period two millennia after the Great Sphinx was erected. Sphinxes did exist in Egyptian mythology, but they were male and benevolent. Some pharaohs chose to commemorate their likeness in Sphinx statue faces, including Hatshepsut, who is considered the only true female pharoah and who often subverted gender expectations in her portraits.

In Greece, on the other hand, the Sphinx was a devious and cruel monster with the head of a woman, body of a lion and wings of a bird. Her name derives from the Greek word for 'squeeze', which might refer to how she killed her victims like a lion – by strangulation. Born in ancient Aethiopia, but sent to Thebes by Hera, the fact that she was both foreign and a woman made her all the more monstrous. She appears frequently as an architectural and artistic motif to ward off evil, especially on funerary monuments. She is perhaps most remembered for her riddles, which she asked passing travellers, strangling and eating those who answered incorrectly.

> The portrayal of female monsters in classical mythology reflects deep-seated ancient misogyny, particularly towards women who wielded power or defied traditional roles. Many of these bigoted attitudes towards women still endure, making the need to understand their mythological origins and deconstruct them all the more important. Several of the female 'monsters' featured in this chapter were simply trying to get on with their lives, quite often following traumatic experiences and violence suffered at the hands of men or gods.
>
> These experiences are now being recognised by women creating art inspired by ancient mythology today. In her song 'FEMININE RAGE' about women in mythology and history, the singer-songwriter PEGGY sings:
>
> 'Each version of the story feels like men get all the glory in the end,
>
> Then we grow up and read about 'em and villainize the victims in our heads.'
>
> Despite their depictions as villains in the past, these so-called monsters have evolved into both survivors of abuse *and* symbols of empowerment, resilience and feminist rage.

Conclusion

As this book has (hopefully) highlighted, women in classical mythology have been used to advance and hinder men's stories by fulfilling the stereotypical roles that men have cast them into. These myths have endured in Western culture, and women have been particularly drawn to their powerful and flawed mythological counterparts, creating art and writing inspired by them since the Medieval period. Today, women and queer people breathe new life into myths and legends without men, producing poetry, novels, art and performances with a distinctly feminist edge and often a camp sensibility. Because histories without men are few and far between, mythology can hold a special place for those who have not been represented, allowing us to draw out our own stories from the lives of fictional women who have become so entrenched in our culture that they almost seem real. Perhaps you have found yourself in one of these characters, or been inspired to reclaim some of their tales to understand more about yourself and the complex and increasingly divided world around us. Either way, the way women's roles in mythology have reflected their role in society has changed over time – where once they served to warn of excessive womanhood, new interpretations of mythology present new possibilities for feminism, helping to legitimise alternatives to traditional femininity and deconstruct outdated ideas about a woman's place. The phrase 'we are the granddaughters of the witches you couldn't burn' has become a feminist mantra, but in a way, we are the descendants of all the women, historical and mythological who blazed the trail for the 'nasty women' and girls, gays, and theys today.

Acknowledgements

I cannot thank Phoebe and the team at Ebury enough! Their patience and support through bad health have been absolutely incredible, and I am so grateful they approached me in the first place and then stuck with me.

I am also thankful to the teams I am and will be working with for international editions of this book, I am absolutely amazed at the response it's had!

Many thanks to my delightful agent Imogen Morrell at Greene & Heaton for having faith in me in the first place.

Plus, thank you to the incredibly talented designers, Double Slice, who have beautifully brought these legends to life.

A big thank you to my parents for encouraging my nerdery and obsession with the ancient world, and taking me to see 'old shit' from a very young age!

Forever thankful to my husbutch Hannah for always believing in and looking after me, even when I don't! Your commitment to always doing the right thing should stir us all to action! Many thanks to your super supportive family, too.

Thank you to our cat sons, Hector and Hephaestus, for giving the best cuddles and helping out by rolling around on my laptop. I genuinely don't know what I would do without my babies!

Extremely appreciative to friends of all genders for cheering me on and responding with such positivity towards this project – I have been overwhelmed by the love from all over the globe! It can be hard having friends spread so far and wide, but moments like these make me realise how lucky I am. Special shout-out to Raspberry Ripples and my fellow disabled queers, although we spend a lot of time being miserable, the care people show one another is constantly inspiring.

To all the women teachers who were patient with me through my chronic illness and undiagnosed neurodivergence, and saw potential, especially my first Classics and Art history teacher, Mrs Hawke.

I am also grateful to my lecturers at Victoria University of Wellington, who helped to ignite a lifelong passion for scholarship and inspired me to pursue classics seriously.

And finally, my PhD Supervisors, Classics and History Faculties and St Hilda's College staff at the University of Oxford for seeing me through complex health issues and providing me with the training, confidence and opportunities to pursue my passion as a career.

A

Achelous 212
Achilles 97, 108, 132, 136
Acropolis 68
Actaeon 79
Aeaea 162, 167
Aeëtes 158
Aegisthus 139
Aeneas 119, 211
Aeschylus
　75, 79, 101, 139, 186, 204
Agamemnon
　132, 134, 136, 139, 190
Agave **21**, 33, 180
Ala-Muki 221
Alecto 185
Allan, Maud 181
Amanirenas 98
Amazons
　91, 93-103, 108, 111, 162
Amnisiades 81
Amphitrite 208
Anatolia 33, 149
Anchises 119
Ancient Egypt
　112-13, 132, 149, 226-7
Ancient Rome
　13, 27, 71, 77, 83-4, 87, 97-8,
　117, 119, 150, 177, 179, 181,
　197, 206, 211-12, 221, 226
Andersen, Hans Christian 219-20
anger/rage, women's 11, 33, 175,
　185, 189, 199, 227
Antiope 96
antisemitism 170
Aotearoa 167
Aphrodite **20**, 29, 51, 85, 93, 108,
　119-24, 131, 133, 142-3, 158,
　183, 186, 192
Apollo 33, 48, 81, 83, 190, 192
Ares 93, 96, 119, 120
Argonauts 108, 109, 182, 211, 214
Ariadne **23**, 57, 183
Ariel 219
Arjuna 105
Artemis 65, 77-81, 83, 96, 106,
　120, 136, 150, 153, 185, 192
Arthurian myth 86-7
Asterion (the Minotaur) 55, 57
Atalanta 91, 106-9, 120, 185
Athena **23**, 44, 51, 65, 67-75, 77,
　83, 119, 131, 141, 164, 186, 200
　see also Minerva
Athens 27, 67-8, 84, 93, 130, 186
Attic War 93
Atwood, Margaret 48, 133
Augustus 98
Aurelian 98

B

Bacchus 179
　see also Dionysos/Dionysus
Barney, Alice Pike 203
Barney, Natalie Clifford 102
bears 80, 106
Bellophoron 224, 225
bestiality 55-7
bisexuality 73, 94, 102, 161
bodies, women's 27, 87, 199
'Bodyguard' 101
bogeywomen 60
Bryher 73
Buyan 86

C

Callimachus 79, 96
Callisto 80
Calydon 108
Calypso 43, 44, 117, 140-3
Camilla 98
Campbell, Donna 167
Carmilla (1872) 143
Cassandra 139, 190-1
Castor 129, 130
castration complex 73
celibacy 65
Celtic myth 220
Cerberus 187, 223
Ceres *see* Demeter
Ceto **20**, 29, 204, 206
Chaos **20**, 29
Charites **23**, 51
Charybdis 208-11
chastity 83-4, 106, 120
Chicago, Judy 30, 102
childbearing 27
childrearing 37
Chimera 223, 224-5
Christianity 60, 87, 169, 171, 217
Chrysaor 202
Circe **23**, 43-4, 140, 142, 147, 149,
　157-8, 162-7, 197, 208, 211, 214
Cithaeron 187
city-states 67, 190
'Classical Reception' 15
Classics 71
clay women 51, 52
Clete 98
Clinton, Hilary 12
Clytemnestra **23**, 43, 75, 117, 126,
　129, 134-9, 186, 190
Corinth 157, 159
Corone 74
Crete 33, 55-7, 81
Cronos **22**, 29, 33, 83, 186
'cross-dressing' 109
crossroads 150, 154
Cybele 33, 120
Cyclopes 29

D

Daedalus 55
Dark Ages 169
Dawn 86-7, 123
Dazhbog (sun god) 86
de Pizan, Christine 71
Deiphobus 132
Demeter **22**, 30, 33, 34-41, 54, 81,
　153, 214
Diana 77, 150
　see also Artemis
Dietrich, Marlene 129
Dionysos/Dionysus 33, 96-7, 119,
　179-80, 183
Disney 147, 192, 219
domestic goddess 61
Dryads 162
Duncan, Isadora 181
Dusk 86-7
Dykes on Bikes (DOB) 189

E

Earth 34, 37
Earth goddesses **20**, 29-30
Echidna **21**, 187, 197, 206, 223
education 71
Eleusinian Mysteries 38
Eleusis 37, 38, 154
emotion
　women's 193
　see also anger/rage; grief
Eos **22**, 123
Epimetheus 51
Erasmus 52, 210
Erechtheion 68
Erinyes *see* Furies
Eris **20**, 131
Eros 117, 123
Eteocles 187
Eumelus 159
Eurasian Steppes 94
Euripides
　55, 79, 132-3, 136, 159, 180
Eurydice 180
Eve 54
evil 51-4, 217, 227

F

familiars 153
feminine archetypes 11-12, 16
　see also femmes fatales;
　homemakers; madwomen;
　monsters; mothers; virgins;
　warriors; witches
feminine skills
　natural 44, 51
　unnatural 44

femininity
  standards of 72, 229
  unacceptable 60, 101, 113, 166, 181, 185, 227
feminists 11, 16, 30, 37, 54, 60-1, 65, 71-2, 74, 79, 102-3, 105, 108-9, 112, 126, 133, 162, 189, 191, 193, 197, 203, 227, 229
femmes fatales 11, 16, 59, 115-43, 164, 203
Fields of Mourning 55
Freud, Sigmund 73
Furies (Erinyes) 29, 185-9

G

Gaia **20**, 29-30, 33, 38, 54, 61, 206
Garbati, Luciano 199
Gellar, Sarah Michelle 143
gender norms 103, 171
gender roles 61, 227
Geoffrey of Monmouth 87
Gigantomachy 85
Glauce 159
Glaucus 165, 208
goddesses **20**, 29-30, 33-41, 44, 51, 55-7, 65, 67-75, 77-81, 83-6, 106, 112-13, 119-24, 129, 131, 141, 149-55, 164, 168, 185-9, 192-3, 204, 206-11, 221
  see also specific goddesses
gods 33, 48, 51-2, 59, 65, 79, 85, 86, 93, 112, 117, 119, 123, 126-9, 141, 161, 162, 179-80, 190-3, 212
  see also specific gods
golden fleece 123, 158
Gorgoneion 200
Gorgons **20**, 29, 73, 197, 204
Goths 98
Graeae **20**, 204, 206
Greek Magical Papyri 150
grief 37, 59-60

H

Hades 33-4, 81, 130, 153, 187, 214
Harrison, Jane 54, 75
Hatshepsut 226
Hatupatu 167, 168
Hauser, Emily 109
Haynes, Natalie 117, 199
H.D. 73
Hecate 149-55, 157
Hecatoncheires 29
Hecuba **23**, 153
Helen of Troy **21**, 117, 119, 126-34, 136, 190
Helios 55, 149, 157
Hephaestus 51, 119, 183, 192
Hera **22**, 33, 59, 80, 119, 120, 131, 158, 159, 192-3, 227

Heracles (Herakles/Hercules) 94, 96
  cattle of 209
Hereaka, Whiti 168
Hermes 48, 51, 119, 141, 164
Hermione **21**, 130
heroes 67, 93, 108, 111, 132
heroines 61, 91, 109, 117, 168
Hesiod 79, 80, 223
Hestia **22**, 33, 65, 83-5
Hinduism 105
Hine-nui-te-pō 168
Hineahuone 52
Hippolutus 93
Hippolyta 93, 96
Hippolytus 120
Hippomenes 108, 120
homemakers 11, 25-61
Homer 209-10
Iliad 93, 97, 119
Odyssey 43-8, 68, 117, 132-3, 140, 197, 211, 214
Homeric Hymn to Demeter 33, 37, 154
homosexuality 15, 73, 171
hope 51-2
Horae (hours) **21**, 51
Hozier 129
Hughes, Molly 189
humanity, downfall 51-4
Hydra 223
Hyginus 208
Hypsipyle 183
hysteria 27, 177

I

Iemanjá 221
Illyria 180
indigenous peoples 221
Indonesia 105
Inuits 221
Iphigenia **23**, 136, 139

J

Jason 94, 108, 109, 120, 132, 158-9, 161, 182, 211, 214
Joan of Arc 91, 109
Josephine, Charlie 109
Juno 211
Jupiter 211

K

Kauffmann, Angelica 166
Kunwinjku 221
Kurangaituku 167-8

L

La Llorona 60
Ladon the dragon 206
Lady Gaga 124
Lamia 59-61, 192
Landon, Letitia 141
Latinus 140
Laurencin, Marie 102
Lawson, Nigella 61
Leda **23**, 126-9, 136
legal status 27
Lemnos 182-3
lesbians 74, 80, 101-3, 109, 143, 168, 171, 181, 189, 199
Lesbos 15
Leto 192
LGBTIQ+ 109
LGBTQ+ 105, 168
LGBTQIA+ 170
Libya 59
Lithuania 86
Lorde 133
Lourdes 87
Lychophron 153
Lyssa 79

M

Māori myth 52, 167-8
Maas, Sarah J. 41
Madonna-Whore complex 87
madwomen 11, 16, 59, 173-93
Maenads 33, 175, 179-81, 190
male domination 11, 37-8, 44, 87
male gaze 199
marriage 27, 55, 60, 108-9, 120, 130, 134-9, 157-61
  rejection 65, 83, 84
Mary (Virgin) 86-7
Meade, L.T. 108
Medea **23**, 108-9, 120, 147, 149, 157-61
Medusa 11-12, 29, 72-3, 197, 199-204, 206, 208, 224
Megaera 185
Mela, Pomponius 87
Melanippe 96
Menelaus 130-3
Mercury 48
mermaids 212-21, 223
Metaneira, Queen 37
Metis 74
#MeToo 191
Mexican folklore 60
Miller, Madeline 57, 162, 166
Minerva 71, 117, 197
  see also Athena
Minos 55, 57
misogyny 52, 175, 177, 217, 227
Mitchell, Anaïs 41

monsters 9, 11, 16, 59–60, 73, 117, 165, 192, 195–227
Moraga, Cherrie 161
Morgen (Morgan le Fay) 87
Morrison, Toni 166
Mother Earth 30, 206
  see also Gaia
mother goddesses 27, 33, 37–8, 61, 65, 120
mothers 27, 34, 59–61, 74–5
  bad 16, 55–7, 65, 157–8, 159, 161
  of evil 51–4
  good 16
  see also stepmothers
Myrmex 74

N

Naiads 162, 208
Nemesis 20, 129
neopaganism 112, 124, 155
Neptune 197
  see also Poseidon
'New Woman' 71
Nightingale, Florence 191
non-binary 109
Norse myth 111, 220
nuns 171
nymphs 20, 23, 65, 77, 80, 81, 149, 158, 162, 165, 197, 208, 211
  see also Calypso
Nyx 20, 187

O

Oceanides 23, 81
Oceanids 149
Oceanus 149
Odysseus 43–4, 47, 67, 117, 119, 132, 134, 140–2, 147, 162, 164, 166, 211–12, 214
olive trees 68
Olympians 51, 67, 77, 85, 150, 193
Olympus 33, 192
Orestes 75, 139, 186
orgasm 177
Orpheus 180, 214
Otrera 93, 96
Ovid 57, 74, 79, 130, 150, 164–5, 190, 193, 204, 214
Oxford University 38, 101

P

paganism 30, 87, 169, 217
  see also neopaganism
Pan 48
Pandora's box 51–4
Paris 119, 130–2, 134, 190, 192
  Judgement of 131

parthenogenesis 29
Parthenon 68
Pasiphaë 23, 55–7, 61
patriarchy 12–13, 72, 108–9, 109, 162, 191, 199
patron deities 44, 67–8, 106, 164, 180
Pegasus 202, 224
PEGGY 227
Peleus 108
Penelope 43–8, 61, 117, 134, 140–1, 147, 211
penis envy 73
Penthesilea 96–8
Pentheus 180
Perse 55, 149
Persephone 23, 34–41, 81, 130, 153, 187, 214
Perseus 199, 200, 204
Persuasion 51
Phaedra 23, 57, 93, 120
pharmakeia 157, 166
Picus, King 164
Pirithous 130
Plath, Sylvia 129
Plutarch 93, 193
Police 210
Pollux 129, 130
Polynices 187
Pompey 98
Poseidon 33, 55, 57, 68, 74, 83, 119, 120, 130, 140, 200, 208–9
  see also Neptune
power 9, 79, 142
powerlessness 27, 142
Pre-Raphaelites 162
pregnancy 27
priestesses 65, 84, 87, 112, 149, 157, 190
Prometheus 51
prophecy 33, 190–1
proto-feminists 72
Psyche 123
Pugh, Florence 175

Q

queer people 15, 77, 80, 101–3, 105, 109, 167–8, 171, 220, 229

R

Ra 112
rape 74, 80, 106, 117, 120, 126, 131, 183, 200
Raukawa iwi 167
Reihana, Lisa 167
Renaissance 52, 162
revenge 79, 112, 120, 123, 147, 164–5, 182–3, 185–6, 192
Rhea 22, 33, 38, 61, 83, 120

Rihanna 199
Riordan, Rick 57, 199
role models, female 9, 65, 81, 105
Rotorua 167
Russia 94
Russian myth 86

S

Sackville-West, Vita 109
Saint, Jennifer 57, 109
saints 109
Salem witches 171
sapphic 72, 80, 94, 199
Sappho 15, 131
Scylla 21, 57, 149, 165, 197, 206, 208–11, 223
sea monsters *see* Ceto; Charybdis; mermaids; Scylla; Sirens
seasons 34
Sedna 221
seductresses 9, 16, 60, 117, 214
Sekhmet 112–13
Selene 22, 77
Selkies 220
sexism 13, 177
sexual assault 11, 199
  see also rape
sexuality, female 57, 133, 164, 171, 199, 214, 220–1
Shakespeare, William 155
Shelley, Mary 41
Shockley, Evie 189
Sirens 197, 203, 212–21
Slavic myth 86–7
Slovenia 86
Smale, Holly 191
Somerville College 38
sorcery 16, 44, 55–7, 120, 157–61, 169
Sparta 67, 126, 130, 136
Sphinxes 21, 203, 223, 226–7
Srikandi/Shikhandi 105
Statius 187
status quo 60
stepmothers 192–3
Stewart, Martha 61
Suffragettes 101

T

takatāpui 168
Tartarus (hell) 29, 150, 187
Taylor, Breonna 189
Te Awekotuku, Ngahuia 168
Telemachus 44
Terra 29–30
  see also Gaia
Tethys 22, 149
Thackeray, William Makepeace 61
Thebes 180, 227

Themiscyra 94
Theseus 93, 94, 96, 130
Thetis 211
Tisiphone 185, 187, 189
Titans **22–3**, 29, 51, 74, 81, 83, 149
trans people 15, 105, 109, 168, 220
triple goddess 150, 154–5
Trivia 150
Trivium 210
Trojan War 43, 97–8, 117, 119, 132, 134, 153, 190
Troy 97, 130, 132, 134, 136, 139, 153, 190, 192, 211
Turkey 94, 97
Tydeus 187
Tyndareus 126

U

Ukraine 86, 94
underworld 33–4, 41, 48, 55, 130, 154, 155, 180, 185, 223
Uranus **20**, 29, 33, 119, 186
Ursa Major 80
uterus 27, 177

V

Valhalla 111
Valkyries 111
vampires 60, 143
Vega, Suzanne 141
Venus 124, 143
  see also Aphrodite
Vergil 97–8, 187
  Aeneid 55, 98, 119, 197, 208, 211, 223
Versace 199
Vesta (Hestia) 84
  see also Hestia
Vestal Virgins 84
Vikings 111
virgins 11, 16, 63–87, 108, 185
Vodou 221
voting rights 65, 71

W

Waller, Constance 108
warriors 11, 16, 89–113, 162
Whitbread, Fatima 108–9
Wicca 30, 124
Wilson, Emily 133, 142
'witch craze' 169–71
witches 11, 16, 55–7, 59–60, 87, 108, 109, 140, 145–71
women's rights 71, 105, 129, 193

Y

Yaksha 105
yawkyawk 221

Z

zagovory 87
Zeus **22**, 33–4, 51, 59, 74–5, 80, 83, 120, 126–9, 131, 141, 158, 192–3, 200, 208–9
Zorya 86

INDEX

Ebury Press, an imprint of Ebury Publishing
Penguin Random House UK
One Embassy Gardens, 8 Viaduct Gdns,
Nine Elms, London SW11 7BW

Ebury Press is part of the Penguin Random House group of companies whose addresses can be found at global.penguinrandomhouse.com

Copyright © Mara Gold 2025

Illustrations © Double Slice Studio (Amelia Leuzzi and Bonnie Eichelberger)

Mara Gold has asserted her right to be identified as the author of this Work in accordance with the Copyright, Designs and Patents Act 1988

Penguin Random House values and supports copyright. Copyright fuels creativity, encourages diverse voices, promotes freedom of expression and supports a vibrant culture. Thank you for purchasing an authorized edition of this book and for respecting intellectual property laws by not reproducing, scanning or distributing any part of it by any means without permission. You are supporting authors and enabling Penguin Random House to continue to publish books for everyone. No part of this book may be used or reproduced in any manner for the purpose of training artificial intelligence technologies or systems. In accordance with Article 4(3) of the DSM Directive 2019/790, Penguin Random House expressly reserves this work from the text and data mining exception.

First published by Ebury Press in 2025

www.penguin.co.uk

A CIP catalogue record for this book is available from the British Library

ISBN 9781529953138

p.227 Lyrics from 'FEMININE RAGE' by PEGGY (2025), used with kind permission of PEGGY

Commissioning Editor: Phoebe Lindsley
Editorial Assistant: Clementine Lussiana
Design: Double Slice Studio (Amelia Leuzzi and Bonnie Eichelberger)
Production: Percie Bridgwater
Publicity and Marketing: Caroline Dowling and Molly Maynard

Colour origination by Altaimage Ltd
Printed and bound in China by C & C Offset Printing Co., Ltd

The authorised representative in the EEA is Penguin Random House Ireland, Morrison Chambers, 32 Nassau Street, Dublin D02 YH68.

Penguin Random House is committed to a sustainable future for our business, our readers and our planet. This book is made from Forest Stewardship Council® certified paper.